PHEEL
the LOVE!

**How the Most Powerful Force in the Universe
Builds Great Companies—Phillie Phanatic Style!**

BY
TOM BURGOYNE AND EVAN MARCUS

Printed in the United States of America
Republished May 2017

Cover Design: S. Preston and Hedy Sirico
Interior Graphics Design: Hedy Sirico
Interior Layout Design: Joseph Martino

For more information on this title please visit:

www.PHEELtheLOVE.com

FANS RAVE *about* PHEEL THE LOVE!

"Everyone knows that the Phillie Phanatic is the Babe Ruth of mascots. This book is proof that the Phanatic is also the Michael Jordan of leadership philosophy. It will inspire you to build great companies by being loving to the people and the organizations you lead."

PAT WILLIAMS
Senior Vice President, Orlando Magic
Author of "Leadership Excellence"

"If you are looking for a book about succeeding in business as well as in life, this is one you cannot afford to pass by."

CHRISTOPHER CHEKOURAS
President & CEO
St. Mary's Health System

"With all the challenges we face today in the world, maybe it's time to embrace the approach that is within us all – the power of love. Taught through the real-life experiences of the Philly Phanatic and leadership guru Evan Marcus, *Pheel the Love!* shows how love can energize customers, engage employees and elevate our lives."

DARYL BREWSTER
President of Nabisco
CEO of Krispy Kreme
CEO of CECP

"If you're interested in being healthier and happier, more productive and more aware of the positive impact we can have on others, then sit back and enjoy the journey!"

RICH GANNON
NFL Analyst on CBS Sports
Former MVP of the NFL

"Love is an essential part of humanity, but it is rarely if ever considered in the context of organizational behavior or strategic thinking. Read this lovely book and get ready to be re-educated about something that can make an extraordinary difference in business and in life. I plan on buying multiple copies and sharing them with my colleagues. I think that CEOs and other organizational leaders would be wise to do the same."

SAM KATZ
Executive Producer
History Making Productions Philadelphia

"Why do I love the Phillie Phanatic? He makes me laugh. Behind that green fur is the best mascot in sports and a heckuva businessman."

KEVIN NEGANDHI
SportsCenter Anchor, ESPN

"What a beautiful recipe for mixing love and passion into the workplace!"

JERALD HARVEY
SVP and Chief Human Resources Officer
Sesame Workshop

"A delightful, insightful, inspiring and touching read. Love is doing the right thing for the right reason."

DENISE KASSEKERT
President
J.W. Hallahan Catholic Girls' High School

"This immensely insightful and enjoyable book cleverly provides the recipe for success in business ventures. All entrepreneurs need to read and embrace this book and its principles."

DR. TOM CASSEL
Professor of Practice and Director
Engineering Entrepreneurship Program,
University of Pennsylvania

"Tom Burgoyne has written many wonderful books about his alter-ego, but none reveals the heart of the Phanatic quite like this one."

ANGELO CATALDI
Morning Show Host
SportsRadio 94WIP

"The iconic Phillie Phanatic reminds us to love the most treasured experiences and moments in life. Tom Burgoyne and Evan Marcus provide us with the courage and insight to create and celebrate these experiences in all we do."

PAUL DUMAS
Chief Human Resources Officer
U.S. Anesthesia Partners

"Pheel The Love! is a happy book, full of love for all."

ALBERT TEGLER, JR.
President and CEO
Tegler McHenry Associates

"There is one person who knows the heart of the Phillie Phanatic better than anyone: Tom Burgoyne."

MICHAEL BARKANN
Comcast SportsNet / SportsRadio 94WIP

"As I talk to many CEOs, the key to success is happy employees who keep customers happy and satisfied. This book speaks to these critical success factors in a novel way. Thank you for writing a book that is entertaining, heart-warming and practical."

DANIEL FITZPATRICK, CFA
President of Citizens Bank of PA/NJ/DE
Head of National Mid-Corporate and Industry Verticals

"Amazing work, and as I read it, I did *Pheel the Love!* The Phanatic's soul is authentic – it's clear to me that there is much more to the Phanatic than whammies, belly whomps and furry hugs. Now Tom and Evan have revealed the secret of the Phanatic's power for all of us to share with our family, friends, co-workers, and fans!"

DAVE RAYMOND
Emperor of Fun and Games
Original Phillie Phanatic

DEDICATION

This book is dedicated to mascots all over the world, who devote their lives to putting smiles on other people's faces.

Mascots are not only found at sports events and dressed in furry, bright-colored costumes. Mascots can be found everywhere, dressed in ordinary clothes.

They are our moms, teachers, neighbors, managers and co-workers. They are people of all walks of life who make the same commitment mascots do – to share the love.

Tom Burgoyne and Evan Marcus

Philadelphia, Pennsylvania
July 4th, 2016

ACKNOWLEDGEMENTS
by Tom

To Mom and Dad – thanks for all your love and support, and for always encouraging me to reach for the stars.

To Jen, Andrew, Dan and Matthew – with all of you in my life, I get to *Pheel the Love!* every day.

To Joe, Ellen, Steve, Mark and Kathy for being the best brothers and sisters a guy could have.

To my Phillies family – it's an honor working for the best organization in sports. I'm thrilled to share this wonderful ride through life with all of you.

To Andrea Guest and Christine Powers - thanks for your friendship and for taking care of our pal, the Phanatic.

A special thanks to S. Preston and Hedy Sirico for their artistic contributions.

To Sue Gordon and Bob Gordon - thank you for helping us with the editing process and for your sage advice. You two are real pros!

To Evan and Tara – meeting you was a blessing and getting to work on this book together has been one of the special joys in my life. Thank you for that gift.

ACKNOWLEDGEMENTS
by Evan

I want to thank my mother and father, Rivian and Harold Marcus. They taught me to be kind and honest.

Ralph Green and Bob Megill are my mentors and friends. They enable me to be the person that I aspire to be. I love you both very much.

Our sons, Dylan, Daniel and Andrew. You are each amazing people. I love being your Daddy. You are the best buddies and teachers I've ever had.

Tom Burgoyne truly is The Phanatic. We have become good friends. Tom is supportive, smart, kind and fun to be with. We work together in the spirit of love, harmony and excellence.

Sometimes I call you: God, Louie, and Source. I am grateful to know that you are loving and caring.

Tara is my best friend. This book does not exist without her. Tom, Tara and I developed these concepts together. Tara lives her life with great integrity and joy. I am grateful that I get to share my life with you and that you love me. I love you!

TABLE *of* CONTENTS

EVAN'S INTRODUCTION

Be Loving.

This is our fundamental message.

If you aspire to be a great leader: be loving.

If you're driven to create a highly profitable, world-class organization: be loving.

If brand loyalty is essential to your business model: be loving.

In this world of fast-paced change, every organization is looking for the critical levers that will ensure their growth and sustainability.

We believe that there is one solution that has been with us since the beginning of time. It is a solution that is rarely, if ever, associated with business. It is a powerful and pragmatic force that is an incredible driver of results. It is…wait for it…love.

Howard Schultz, the iconic CEO of Starbucks, left that position in 2000 but returned eight years later. Many think he came back because of the downturn in the organization, but that was not the case. After reading his book, *Onward* and watching many of his interviews, one thing became clear to us. He came back because of love.

As a business leader, wouldn't you love to have your company overflowing with smart, dedicated people who love your organization as much as Howard Schultz loves Starbucks? Love is a huge competitive

1

advantage in the marketplace and will set you on a path to being a great company.

You may think that infusing the power of love into your current workplace is impossible. We think the exact opposite.

Pheel the Love!™ will show you how to create this love in a most unexpected way: with the help of a big, green bird from the Galapagos Islands, a character better known as the Phillie Phanatic. You may wonder what the mascot of the Philadelphia Phillies has to do with your business success. We believe everything.

For those who may not be aware, the Phillie Phanatic is recognized as the most popular and beloved mascot in *all* of sports – not just baseball. He is consistently the number one seller of merchandise for the Phillies – exceeding the sales of even the most popular players. His tremendous success in the gift shop is a natural by-product of the love his fans have for him.

We share this message of love through the lens of the Phanatic and my friend Tom Burgoyne, the man who has been the mascot for close to 30 years, because, as you will soon learn, this is how the message came to us.

As a consultant, I've worked with companies in a wide range of industries from health care to construction, from financial services to universities. I've worked with very large organizations and very small ones – and love has a place in every one of them.

If you want to understand the business case for love – the hard, cold facts – here they are. First, stock prices for companies that are listed on Fortune Magazine's annual 100 Best Places to Work List consistently outperform peer companies not on the list by about 2-1. That fact, in and of itself, is huge. But wait, there is more. Companies on this list also perform better in the following areas:

- ✓ More discretionary effort - employees who feel loved and valued will often give more than what's expected of them.

- ✓ Love breeds loyalty - if you love your employees, your employees will in turn, love your customers.

- ✓ Safety - safety records are better when employees love their employer.

- ✓ Reputation - companies that are great to work for generate buzz and attract quality people.

It goes without saying that you'll love being loving even more when you see it improving your metrics in all of these areas!

If you choose to read on, we will explain how love is already a driving force behind many great organizations. We will teach you how to use love to improve key drivers of success like operational excellence, customer loyalty and quality. You'll begin to see how people, products, processes and profits reach their fullest potential when they are fueled by love principles.

Aiming for the fences, our vision is for love to become a foundational concept in business and a driver of traditional business practice. We want love embedded in the heart and soul of business strategy, tactics and operations. Crazy we know, but we foresee love being prominent in the mission, vision and values of every organization. The business world touches each one of us every day. It is the perfect proving ground to realize the potential of love. Just remember how the Phillie Phanatic spreads love, while consistently generating terrific sales year-after-year.

If you really want your business to thrive, why pass up on the opportunity to tap into the most powerful force in the universe?

TOM'S INTRODUCTION

I love being the Phillie Phanatic.

People say to me all the time, *"You have the greatest job in the world."* How can I argue? I get to dress up in a green, funny costume and cheer on the Phillies at every home game. As the Phanatic, I goof around with our players and get into it with the opposing team. I dance with coaches, goose umpires and lead cheers from the dugout. It's a dream come true.

Personally, being a mascot for a living isn't that much of a stretch. Growing up in the suburbs of Philadelphia, I was the class clown. I used to love making my friends laugh. If that meant staying after school in detention or having to write, *"I should not jam pencils up my nose"* 500 times as a punishment, so be it. So my path has been consistent. As the Phanatic, I get to make the fans laugh, but without the punishment – or the pain of having six pencils crammed up my nose.

Speaking of pain, my job as a mascot isn't always all fun and games. I've had my share of bumps, bruises and broken bones along the way. There are some other drawbacks as well. Most of the time, the costume can smell worse than a petting zoo at low tide. On hot summer days, the heat inside the costume makes me sweat enough to fill an army canteen. Sometimes, fur balls the size of marshmallows get lodged in my throat, making the simple act of breathing a luxury. For me, dehydration is a way of life.

But who's complaining? I still wouldn't trade my job for anything in the world. I have rubbed elbows with celebrities and jumped up on stage with rock stars. I've danced with baseball legends. I've spent a weekend in Cooperstown when the Phanatic was enshrined in Baseball's Hall of Fame. I've led parades, dangled from helicopters and camped out on billboards. I've crashed weddings and bar mitzvahs, and on one memorable night, performed for the nine Supreme Court justices at a private dinner. As the Phanatic, I've been featured on national TV shows, filmed commercials and have popped up on ESPN's SportsCenter hundreds of times. I've had videos go viral on YouTube and have been impersonated on Facebook. I've appeared in ballparks around the country and travelled all over the world bringing the Phanatic's special brand of humor to sports fans everywhere. It's a life that I dreamed about as a kid and it's a life and feeling that I wish every Philadelphia sports fan could somehow experience at least once in their lives: to be the Phanatic for just one day.

Because if you were to step into the Phanatic's oversized green sneakers, you would see the same thing that I see when people come face to snout with the big green guy. You'd see the giddiness, joy and excitement every day. And I'm not just talking about kids. I've seen women weep with joy and grown men turn into little boys right before my eyes. They chase after the Phanatic with their children in tow because that's what they did when they were kids. Teenage girls gush over the Phanatic and rush over to him to snap a selfie for their Instagram page. At times, I feel like one of the Beatles being chased down the street by adoring crowds at the height of their popularity, with the difference being that John, Paul, George and Ringo never had to wear a 35-pound green shag carpet for a living.

It seems that no matter where the Phanatic goes, smiles, laughter and yes – love – greet him. After 28 years of performing as one of the most recognized mascots in sports, I brushed off that reaction as nothing out of the ordinary. Doesn't everybody get attacked by screaming fans every time they go to work?

One day, my co-author, Evan, came to the ballpark to follow me around at a Phillies game. It was a typical night of hugs, high-fives, posing for pictures and general hysteria. Evan followed me to my dressing room, where I go to take off my head (the Phanatic's head, not *my* head) and take a break. He looked at me like I had three heads – not just two.

"Tom, that was crazy out there!"

"Just another day at the office, Evan."

Over the next few weeks, Evan and I met to talk about my job and the positive effect it has on people. We realized that no, not everyone gets chased by adoring fans when they go to work, but that feeling of excitement and passion can exist if you approach every day as though *you* were the Phanatic. And all facets of your life – your personal life, your business life and the lives of everyone you touch – will be richer and fuller... just without the smell.

How does the Phillie Phanatic approach life every day? In two words: Be Loving.

Evan and I believe that by being loving, you'll not only bring the love the Phanatic brings to everyone you meet each day, but you'll receive the love the Phanatic receives every day.

Maybe the Phanatic *is* the fifth Beatle or maybe he was hanging out in the studio during the recording of the Abbey Road album. The Beatles recorded the song, "The End" for that album. It was the last song they ever recorded together and it finished with the idea that the love you give is the love you get.

The Phillie Phanatic would agree. Rock on!

PART I

THE CASE *for* LOVE

CHAPTER 1

ORCHESTRATED *by* LOVE

Evan: I got a call one day from Tom Iacovone. Tom is head of the Trade Show and Events division at Art Guild, a high-end trade show and design company. Art Guild was planning an event to thank their customers. Tom Iacovone was considering me to deliver a keynote to kick-off the event. We talked a few times and I enjoyed my conversations with Tom very much. Even though we had never met, he spoke to me like a friend. The engagement looked promising. Then, out of the blue, Trade Show Tom called with bad news. His partner happened to be friends with the brother of the Phillie Phanatic. Trade Show Tom and his partners decided to have the guy who plays the Phanatic deliver the keynote. I couldn't believe that I was getting bumped by a big, green, goofy mascot.

Trade Show Tom is a good guy. Even though I wasn't chosen to speak, he invited me to come to the event as his guest. He offered me a booth as a way to promote our company. His customers are all Fortune 500 companies and he hoped I could make some good connections. He genuinely wanted to help me out, which surprised me, as I was someone he barely knew.

When I arrived at the tradeshow, I was personally greeted by Trade Show Tom. He treated me like his most important customer. He introduced me to people like I was a celebrity. This really touched me. Over the years, I've gotten to know Tom Iacovone much better and have come to realize that this is how Tom treats everyone. And it's why so many people love Tom Iacovone and why his customers and staff are so loyal to him.

At that time, we had not yet formalized our love principles, but Tom Iacovone was demonstrating them to me. And he was the perfect partner to orchestrate my serendipitous meeting with Tom Burgoyne. As you will see in this story, all of the players were motivated by love. We were about to experience the magnificent results that being loving brings.

I went into the ballroom to hear the Phanatic's talk. Tom Iacovone introduced Tom Burgoyne, the Phanatic's "Best Friend." I thought that this might be a good opportunity for me to learn something that would help me deliver my keynotes, so I took out my iPhone and started taking notes.

Phanatic Tom started telling great stories about his life in costume. The audience sat enthralled, enjoying the backstage view of this incredibly likeable and popular mascot.

I enjoyed his stories very much. But there was something missing for me. I sensed that there was a bigger message underlying his stories. I suspected that the message was inside Tom and that there was more to him than the stories themselves. I had a genuine and pure desire to help him, and as you are about to see, Tom Iacovone had a genuine desire to help Tom B. and me.

After the talk was over, Tom Iacovone gave both Tom Burgoyne and me a gift. He introduced us to each other. I told Tom B. that I enjoyed his talk. Then I went against my own rule of *"don't give advice unless someone asks for it"* and told Tom B. that I had some thoughts I wanted to share with him about ways to improve his talk.

My offer to help him was timely. Tom was starting to step out of the costume and do more public speaking appearances as himself. He wanted to take his talk to another level and he readily accepted my offer.

We set a date and I showed up at the Phanatic's "office" with my trusted post-it pad and pens. I asked him to re-tell me a bunch of his stories. As he did, we wrote the essence of each story on a sticky note and organized them into common themes. From this process, the larger meaning behind his message emerged. It felt like we just hit a home run.

After my meetings with Tom, Tara, my wife and business partner could see the excitement in me. She felt that there might be something more there, not just creating a stronger keynote for Tom, but something we could do together.

At our first joint meeting, Tom started telling Tara some of the stories about his life as the Phanatic. As Tom talked, we thought about how all of his stories and life experiences tied together. We met a few more times, sharing coffee, stories and laughs, but had a hard time coming up with a core message for a keynote or workshop that worked for all of us.

At our third or fourth meeting, Tom showed up a few minutes late. That was unusual since being early is the equivalent to being on time for Tom. He was coming from lunch with his family and he casually told us that the waitress at the restaurant had discovered that he was the Phillie Phanatic.

Tom's fame is unusual. While dressed as the Phanatic everyone knows him, but as Tom, he's anonymous. On this day, the waitress discovered Tom's alter ego. Being "discovered" happens often enough that when the waitress came to the table with her enthusiastic recognition, Tom's family rolled their eyes, *"Here we go again."* Tom chuckled as he recalled the waitress' reaction. She kept repeating, *"Oh my God, I love the Phanatic. I really love the Phanatic!"*

And in that moment, a flash came to me. That's it! LOVE!

In all of Tom's stories, we kept hearing about love. *"I love the Phanatic!"* We heard and saw it over and over again. People are fanatically in love with the Phanatic. We took a group of executives to the ballpark to meet Tom and hear his story. Some of the women wore Phanatic earrings and Phanatic t-shirts. Even the men got googly-eyed when they met him.

Every time I am out with Tom, I'm amazed at the giddy reaction people have when they find out that he is the Phillie Phanatic. Recently we gave a talk to a local group of business leaders. The room was filled with some heavy hitters so I wasn't sure what their level of love for the Phanatic would be. Instead of asking, *"Who here loves the Phanatic?"* I sheepishly asked, *"Who here likes the Phanatic?"* The room almost rebelled against me. They jumped up, *"Like the Phanatic? We LOVE the Phanatic!"* they screamed. Again, it was the word love.

When Tom told us about the waitress, the light bulb went off. This was the message we were looking for! What company doesn't want their customers to love them with the same fervor and enthusiasm that folks love the Phanatic? We were so excited. It felt like a great discovery. Love was our "hook", except it wasn't a hook. It was genuine. We felt like we had discovered the Holy Grail and it was love!

In business, organizations are always looking for a unique selling proposition, something that makes them stand out from their competitors – something that will ensure their future viability. When competitors can easily match both your product and your price, what is left? What helps create a thriving future? The answer in a nutshell is loyalty: loyalty from your team and loyalty from your customers. Loyal customers are really hard to steal. (Think of a company or service you are loyal to; what would it take you to leave?) Loyal, engaged employees will be super committed to ensuring your organizations' success. And when a really talented member of your team – one who feels loved and appreciated – is being wooed by a head hunter to work somewhere else, how likely is he or she to leave?

So how do you achieve this level of love and loyalty?

That's exactly the question we asked ourselves. We wanted and needed to take a closer look at the love the Phanatic generated to see if there was any "secret sauce" that could be replicated.

Our investigation revealed seven principles that create this kind of love, and it became clear to us that these principles were universal. Most important, they could be applied in a business setting.

Once we figured out the principles, we decided to create a keynote and workshop combination to teach these principles. We called the program *Loyal, Loving Fans for Life!*™. When we first named it, Tom asked, *"Why doesn't the word love come first?"* The honest answer is because we were afraid. We were afraid that if we used the word love our clients would not take us seriously. As we started delivering the program, we came to see and believe that love is the critical word and that our audience was not afraid of it. In fact, they gravitated to it. At one of our workshops, Kevin Bender, the former head of retail operations for Aramark at Citizens Bank Park (where the Phillies play) confirmed that for us. We had asked the question, *"Can we make the business case for love?"* *"You absolutely can!"* he said. He went on to say that the top three best-selling items were Phanatic merchandise. *"Anything we put the Phanatic's image on sells. He is our best player. He never has a bad year, never gets traded and everyone loves him."* Evidence like Kevin's and the response of our attendees started to give us the courage to embrace the word love. If we created the program anew, I trust we'd call it *Loving, Loyal Fans for Life!*

Pheel the Love! is intended for leaders of organizations. In the traditional sense, leaders have certain titles: CEO, President, Vice President, Chief Officer, Director and Manager. But we want to expand that definition. Leadership in our experience is not solely a function of title or role – leadership can and should come from everyone. Anyone who is willing to model the highest aspirations and values of an organization is a leader in our view.

This book is written as a conversation between Tom and myself because this is how we created it – through conversation.

It's our hope that after reading this book, you will have the courage and confidence to implement these principles in your company. We want more people and more organizations to benefit from *Pheeling the Love!*

CHAPTER 2
FUELED *by* LOVE

Tom: Do you like the movie *Titanic*?

Evan: Love it!

Tom: If you love *Titanic* Evan, then you will remember this line, *"I'm king of the world!"*

That's what Leo DiCaprio's character Jack yells while standing on the edge of the infamous ship, staring out into the wild Atlantic Ocean, his arms flung wide, pretending to take flight. Just days before, Jack was in a grimy bar in Southampton, England, drinking beer and playing cards. Now he was on his way to America on the most luxurious ocean liner in the world and reveling in his good fortune.

"I'm king of the world!"

That's exactly how I felt on October 22, 1980. I wasn't propped up on the bow of the ship like Jack. No, I was standing on a 28,000-pound statue called "Triune" doing my best not to fall off. Like Jack, what lay before me was one of the most beautiful sights I had ever seen – at least to a 15-year-old Philly sports junkie like me. It wasn't the vastness of the Atlantic staring back at me. No, this was better. I was looking out at the sea of people who filled Center City Philadelphia on the day of the Phillies 1980 Championship Parade. They say over a million people cut school, called in sick and took an early vacation that day to celebrate the first World

19

Series victory in the city's history. People were everywhere. Fans lined up twenty to thirty deep in the streets around City Hall. Crazies, like me, were dangling from trees and lampposts and standing on the tops of parked cars. They congregated on rooftops and peered out windows just trying to get a glimpse of the world champs.

As I waited for the 18-wheelers carrying the players to roll past, I counted my blessings and pinched myself repeatedly to make sure I wasn't dreaming. I had been a loyal, loving Phillies fan since the first time I saw them play in person. That date was April 10, 1971 and it was the first Opening Day ever at the now razed Veterans Stadium.

When I saw the stadium for the first time, I couldn't believe how big it was. It had orange and yellow seats and bright, green, plastic grass called AstroTurf. There were "dancing" water fountains that shot water into the sky behind the outfield fence after a Phillies player hit a homerun, and two gigantic scoreboards that flashed funny animations throughout the game. Just before the game started, catcher "Irish" Mike Ryan caught the ceremonial first ball that was dropped from a helicopter. The first Phillies season in the Vet's history had begun.

And so, too, had my love affair with the Phillies.

Actually, I wasn't just a Phillies fan. I loved all the Philly sports teams, especially the Julius Erving-led Sixers. I plastered my walls with Dr. J posters and collected every magazine cover that he graced. I'd stay up to watch the away games on TV and listen to the home games on the radio. I had a black school bag that resembled a doctor's medical bag with the words "Doctor J's Bag" emblazoned in white on the side. Day after day, I played basketball in the driveway after school until dark, trying to perfect the Doctor's patented finger roll.

When the basketball season ended, the baseball season was just getting under way. Of course, I played baseball as a kid – we all did. It was exciting just waiting for the snow to melt and spring to arrive. There is nothing quite like the smell of freshly mowed grass, blooming flowers and a leather baseball glove. It's a smell that lingers with me even to this day and transports me back to my happy place.

When I wasn't playing with my organized team, my friends and I would play pick-up games in the park or Wiffle ball in the school yard. I perfected my Harry Kalas *"Outa Here"* home run call at an early age and would announce every home run that someone would hit. I attended our baseball organization's banquet every year where star players like Tug McGraw and Tim McCarver would be invited to speak and sign autographs. The banquets always ended the same way: a projector and movie screen were set up and we would watch the Phillies highlight film with the booming, god-like voice of John Facenda narrating all the action.

My Dad knew how big a fan I was. He was in the printing business and was able to get a copy of the

Phillies yearbook before it was officially released. I'd wait for the day he'd come home with the new yearbook, and along with my brothers and sisters, pour over every page.

And now, there I was, ditching school with my three buddies, balancing at the top of a bronze sculpture, waiting for my heroes from those yearbook pages to come rolling past on flatbed trucks through a sea of Phillies fans.

The roar was deafening as the caravan approached. Travelling east down Market Street, the trucks appeared and inched their way through the crowd. Slowing down even more, they made the turn around City Hall where our statue was situated. The players waved, pumped their fists and flashed the "We're #1" sign. Tugger, Larry Bowa, Pete Rose, Mike Schmidt, the "Bull" Greg Luzinski, Bob Boone, Garry Maddox, "Lefty" Steve Carlton and all the rest were there. It was pandemonium! After the caravan passed, we climbed down from the statue to follow the parade. Our goal was to get to JFK Stadium (also now gone!) to watch the ceremony, so we ran parallel to Broad Street on 15th street, and hopped in the back of a pick-up truck the rest of the way to the 100,000 seat stadium.

We made it inside the stadium just as the players were arriving – perfect timing! We were there when Harry Kalas welcomed everyone to the party and we laughed out loud when Tugger, holding a copy of the Philadelphia Daily News with the headline *"We Win"* over his head, announced to the jubilant crowd

"New York can take this championship and STICK IT!" It was, indeed, the perfect day.

The joy I felt that day and the passion I have for the Phillies and Philly sports has always been in me. It is genuine and can't be fabricated. I think that is why I love being the Phillie Phanatic. I am tapping into something that I really loved as a kid.

I was in seventh grade in 1978 when the Phanatic made his debut. At the time, my true loves were Philly sports, Mad magazines and the Three Stooges. The Phanatic was all of those wonderful things wrapped up into one big, funny, green fur ball. Whenever my family and I went to a Phillies game, I was captivated by the Phanatic roaming the stands or dancing around the field. I loved it every time we went to the Vet, but I went to watch not just the Phillies – but the Phanatic, too.

Now, imagine what it would be like if we could experience all of those feelings of passion and excitement for the things we loved as kids now, with one flip of a switch. It would be amazing! Imagine turning on those emotions any time we wanted. For me, sitting in the 700 level at the Vet with my family, watching the Phillies and the Phanatic, was the best. You may have other memories you'd like to tap to *Pheel the Love!* Maybe you love another team as much as I love the Phillies (don't worry, I forgive you). For some, it might be the memory of reading a good book, playing with your friends after school, watching a great movie or TV show, or getting together with your family around the holidays. That is the love, the passion and the feeling we want you to have every day. When that kind of passion burns inside you, when that kind of love fills your heart, you really do feel like you are *"king of the world"!*

Evan: This is great, Tom. One of the first things I realized in trying to understand Phanatic-style love was how much love you have for sports and goofy humor. You are a huge fan.

Tom: I'm not sure you can generate the love we are talking about if you don't love what you do in your heart and soul.

Evan: It's not only love for what you do, but a love for the product, service, and industry that you represent.

Tom: That's correct. It was that passion that led me to become the Phillie Phanatic, and continues to fuel my life as the Phanatic today.

I attended high school at St. Joseph's Prep in Philadelphia. Their mascot is the Hawk. Traditionally, the Prep inherited the old stinky feathery hand-me-down costume from St. Joe's University, whose mascot is also the Hawk. But finally, my senior year, the school invested in its own costume. This new costume was more of a cartoon version of the Hawk and they needed the right personality to fill it…someone a little goofy, someone who was part sports fan, part class clown. Guess who the students chose?

The point is, my classmates saw in me the qualities that led them to want me to be their mascot.

Evan: This is one of our key discoveries. The love has to be genuine and true to who you are as a person. Here's an example. Growing up, I did not like to read. It's hard to believe, but in all my years of school, I only ever read one book cover-to-cover, *The Legend of Dr. J.*

Like you, I loved Dr. J. He was the best, most exciting basketball player of his day and he was leaving the old ABA and taking his talents to the NBA. I can still remember how I felt the morning I saw this news chronicled in the headlines of our newspaper. The great Doctor J was going to be a Seventy-Sixer.

Wow! I loved watching Doc, talking about Doc, thinking about Doc. He played with great flare, power and grace. He was a good guy. He rallied the troops. The players loved Dr. J. He made us all believe.

I was not the only one who loved Dr. J. Lots of people did. Tom loved "The Doc" even more than I did. He told me that his whole room was plastered with Doc stuff. Of course, we all wanted some piece of The Doc to show some connection to him. So when his book came out, even though I didn't like to read, I couldn't wait to read it. I read every word.

How does this relate to our theory of love? Think of everything you do on a daily basis to grow and manage your business. Imagine you could do those things with the same fervor and passion that Tom has about being the Phillie Phanatic or that I had about reading *The Legend of Dr. J.*

Imagine going to work fueled by love: you'd be unbeatable!

CHAPTER 3
TALKIN' *about* LOVE

The key to unleashing the full power of love in organizations is talking about it out loud. Rather than trying to dictate what love is, we are interested in getting people discussing it in meetings, in daily conversations, whenever possible – because the more we talk about love, the more love grows. So, let's have a conversation. The question is, *"How would you define love?"*

Evan's Definition

I wanted to run away from answering this question. Trying to define love is a Herculean task.

I'm sure if we put a hundred people in a room and asked them what love is, we would get a hundred different responses. The cool thing is that we can each have our own understanding of love.

Here's my definition:

"Love is the force that unleashes our fullest potential."

This idea of unleashing potential is very important to Tara and me. The mission for our company is to "Unleash the fullest potential of everyone on the planet, creating a ripple effect that changes the world." It's a big statement we know, but we figured, why not? It's worth failing at.

Although love may be hard to define, we all know it when we see it. Our company runs a group called the Sounding Board™. Our Sounding Board is comprised of C-level executives who are interested in upping their game. A large part of what the Sounding Board does is visit leaders of great organizations to learn what makes them great.

A few years back, we spent the better part of a day with Jack Bogle, the iconic founder of the wildly successful investment company called Vanguard. Many would argue that Vanguard's success is due, in large part, to its approach of being loving to their customers. Jack told the story of how they came upon the idea for the now famous index mutual fund. He said that what attracted him to this concept was his regard for his customers, and his desire to put their needs first. The index fund promised greater returns for smaller fees. Jack was concerned that many investment professionals were taking too much money out of the pockets of the investors. He was looking for a way to provide a fairer value to his customers. He demonstrated one element of the DNA of love (more on that soon) by noticing the needs of others.

On a personal note, while we were waiting in the lobby to meet Mr. Bogle, his administrative assistant was attending to us. She was an older woman with a kind and lively spirit. We spent some time making small talk and it was then that she whispered to a few of us, *"I've had cancer three times in my life and*

each time after I recovered, Jack took me back."
You couldn't miss the love and loyalty in her eyes.

Tom's Definition

Evan: Tom, were you a fan of professional wrestling when you were growing up?

Tom: Absolutely!

Evan: Who was your favorite? Haystacks Calhoun or Gorilla Monsoon?

Tom: No way, Andre the Giant!

Evan: In the spirit of the great tag team wrestling duos, it's my turn to tap out. You're on.

Tom: What is love? That's a pretty heavy question. Normally, philosophers and theologians are the ones tackling that question, not mascots. But since Evan took a crack at it – and defined love beautifully, I might add – I'll bite.

When I think of the word love and what it means, I think about a question that I get asked all the time.

"What do you love most about your job?"

Most people think the best part of my job is getting to go to every Phillies game without ever having to pay for a ticket. Some might guess the best part is riding around the field on my ATV or getting the chance to meet the players. And while those are some of the reasons I love my job, the *best* part is getting to see people at their best every day.

As the Phanatic, I'm fortunate enough to witness the goodness of people everywhere I go. That might sound corny, but it's the truth. I know that in today's world, it can be hard to find daily examples of love. But when I'm dressed in that green, furry costume, love is everywhere. Every time the Phillies open the gates and the fans come streaming in, I get to see love in action. Mom, Dad and the kids put their lives on hold for a few hours, and spend time together as a family to root on the home team. Young couples flirt between innings and older couples hold hands as they stroll along the concourse. Communities buy tickets and cheer as one from the upper deck. Many buy tickets through the Phillies fund-raising program, raising money for great causes.

On most nights, we have choirs sing the national anthem. These groups are wide-eyed and excited as they walk onto the field for the first time. I can feel the love and sense of pride they have as they faithfully sing the national anthem each night. Before the game, we usually highlight individuals on the field who have had a positive impact in the community. These people help other people. For these folks, love comes naturally. While their accomplishments are read over the PA system, their face are shown on our gigantic video screen while the Phanatic gives them a hug.

I also feel the love when I see the passion of our fans. They come to the ballpark, day in and day out, decked out in Phillies gear and follow the team through good times and bad times. I see the starry-eyed look of wonderment of kids seeking autographs before the game. It's the same pure love and enthusiasm that filled my heart as a kid when I was following the Phillies.

The Phanatic is a professional party-goer. Love is in the air when the Phanatic barges in on a wedding reception, bar mitzvah or retirement party. Crashing these parties is a blast. At these celebrations, everyone is already pumped up and has had a cocktail or two by the time the Phanatic arrives. When the Phanatic makes his big entrance, "loving" mayhem ensues. Weddings in particular can be especially crazy. To cause additional chaos, I ask the DJ to make an announcement, *"Ladies and gentlemen, I don't want to alarm you but Betty's old boyfriend* (Betty is the bride) *has just arrived and he's causing a scene in the lobby. He said that he will leave without further incident if he can get one final dance with his old girlfriend."* By now, the crowd is hushed and whispering amongst themselves. *"Can it be? Did Tony* (the ex-boyfriend) *really have the nerve to show up here TODAY?"* After an uncomfortable pause and tension in the air, the Phanatic makes his grand entrance, lays a mega-kiss on the bride and invites everyone out onto the dance floor.

I really get to see love at its best when the Phillie Phanatic is out and about in the community. Everywhere I go, I see dedicated people working together to make the world a better place. Parades are a great example. Everyone loves a parade, including the Phanatic. He'll hang off a truck blowing kisses and rolling his belly down the parade route. As much fun as I have at a parade, I know that it takes a year's worth of planning to pull-off a successful parade. I marvel at the commitment from ordinary working folks who plan these types of community events. Nobody is getting paid. People give up what little time they have in their busy lives to purposely spread the love.

Youth baseball and other youth sports wouldn't exist if there weren't dedicated adults organizing the leagues, raising money and maintaining the fields. The Phanatic attends beef and beer fundraisers. These heart-warming events raise money for neighbors who need help paying their medical bills or for those struggling to make ends meet after losing a spouse. 5K runs and charity walks sprout up in the spring and fall months like clockwork. These events draw thousands of people, raise money and awareness for great causes and help bring people together for a common goal. Charity golf events, summer camps, church carnivals, military homecomings, schools, nursing homes, and hospitals - everywhere the Phanatic goes, people are helping other people, defining what it means to love.

Love is people at their best. It's having the passion and desire to lift an individual or community up, to make the world a better place.

It's selflessly and consistently placing the needs of our neighbors, family, friends and co-workers ahead of our own needs. It's caring for others. The ripple effect is that it makes us feel good. When we can make a positive impact on another person's life, we are being the best we can be. As leaders, we want people operating at their best and highest selves. When people live with the intent of love in their hearts, they can lift the entire team, the entire organization, to unlimited heights.

A Broader Definition of Love

We are redefining a word that has become synonymous with romantic notions, and as such, has lost much of its broader power.

By talkin' about love, we deepen our understanding of the word and unleash its ability to produce results.

When is the last time you saw the word love prominent in a mission statement or an annual report? We foresee business leaders purposely infusing their organizations with love. We want boards of directors to understand the undeniable power of love to move their missions forward.

We imagine leaders embracing the word love and using it freely because it will help them achieve their goals. We envision love in all forms of leadership: politicians talking about love on the campaign trail, principals and teachers advocating for more love in our schools, police officers and citizens being more loving to each other.

We want the word love to be as ubiquitous in business vernacular as the words "market share" and "profitability." We imagine strategic plans embracing love concepts. And we firmly believe that when leaders champion this message of love and incorporate it into their business plans, love won't only be happening between the bedsheets, it will have a prominent and promising place on the spreadsheets.

CHAPTER 4

NOTHING *trumps* LOVE!

Repeat after me and say, *"I LOVE it!"* Go ahead – say it again with all the gusto you would summon up for something you really love: *"I LOVE it!"*

Notice the tone of your voice, the energy in your body and the clarity in your declaration. *"I LOVE it!"* *"I really LOVE it!"*

Now try it again, except this time, substitute the word "love" for the word "like". Say, *"I like it!"*

How does that feel? Not nearly as good as, *"I love it!"*, right?

You can replace the word "love" in that sentence with any other word and they will all fall short. Why? Because *nothing* trumps love.

If nothing trumps love, then wouldn't it make sense to learn how to harness its power?

We are big fans of a strategy called Appreciative Inquiry (AI). AI (not to be confused with hall of fame Philly hoops star Allen Iverson) was conceived by David Cooperider. It is based on a very simple concept that asserts that what we focus upon grows. If we are trying to positively impact organizations, we should focus on what is working. In the traditional consulting mindset, we identify what's not working, and try to fix it. Here's the problem with that approach – it's a bottomless pit. There will always be more to fix. And if "what we focus upon grows" is true, then focusing on what isn't working will create more stuff that doesn't work.

AI is a simple tool to use. It is based on story telling. People share stories of success, then analyze their stories to uncover the root causes of that success. And here's why this technique is so powerful. The root causes of personal success don't just apply to one specific story. They are universal. The root causes, whether found in one or several stories, can be applied to any situation. Once we know the root causes of success, we can apply these principles in a broad range of situations.

In conducting research for *Pheel the Love!*, we used AI to help us better understand the root causes of love. We started looking at situations where people would say, *"I love it!"* to understand the reasons why. (By the way, you can play this game too. Just ask yourself, *"What do I absolutely love?"* Then write down the reasons you feel that way.) We've provided a few examples. Our lead-off batter is, of course, the Phillie Phanatic.

I LOVE the Phillie Phanatic!

It takes something special to be the best in any profession, activity or endeavor. The Phillie Phanatic is consistently voted the number one mascot in all of baseball. Talk to any Philadelphia sports fan or any fan who is familiar with the Phillie Phanatic and you will hear the phrase, *"I love the Phanatic!"* over and over again. But exactly why do people love him so much? Let's examine some of the reasons why:

> **Root Causes of "I Love the Phanatic!"**
>
> - He's funny and makes me laugh.
> - He's always upbeat and lifts my spirits.
> - He makes me feel loved and special.
> - He makes me feel like anything is possible.
> - He is pure positive energy – he represents the best of what I can be.
> - He has been around for a long time and connects me to great memories.
> - He is a great dancer and makes me want to dance.
> - He is loyal to his team, the Phillies.
> - He appeals to people young and old.
> - He is a wonderful representative and ambassador for Philadelphia.
> - He cares and supports great causes – like encouraging kids to read.
> - He is tall, green and handsome!

Wouldn't you want your customers to have this kind of love and loyalty for you? Here's another example:

I LOVE My Job!

Tom and I were at a business conference and met a woman who told us a story about her husband who was an attorney. He had just started a new job. During his job search, she encouraged him to find a firm with a great culture. She was wise enough to know that the environment in which he worked would have a huge impact on the quality of his work and his life. He found a firm that felt "just right." It turned out to be a great decision. She commented on how much he loves it there. Loving his place of work also has side benefits, she said, in that he is more present at home, and is a better father and a better husband. He attributes it all to the fact that he loves his job and has a sense of fulfillment that he's never had with any other firm.

Here are some of the reasons why people love their jobs:

Root Causes of Why "I LOVE my Job!"

- I feel appreciated and important.
- My colleagues respect my opinion.
- I understand what is expected of me.
- I have what I need to do my job.
- My co-workers are smart, dedicated, nice people.
- The work allows me to be creative and apply my skills.
- I am learning a lot.

- There is a lot of collaboration, people just chip in and help each other.
- We do excellent work.
- Every aspect of our company is really special – from the way the place looks to how we answer our phones.
- Our commitment to customer service is amazing; the way we take care of our clients is fantastic.
- We operate ethically.
- Our customers love working with us.
- I'm proud to be part of this company.

When we say we love our work, it is a short form for saying all or many of these things reflected in this list. It is clear that these elements can serve as clues towards creating a great place to work.

Let's try AI again with something familiar to most of us – think of a restaurant you love. Why do you love it?

Root Causes of "I Love this Restaurant!"

- The atmosphere was warm and friendly.
- The food was amazing.
- The presentation of the food was beautiful.
- The chef came out and said hello to us.
- The price was reasonable.
- We felt special.

Appreciative Inquiry Applied

There are two parts to using this approach to make any situation more loving. The first is buying into the belief that nothing trumps love. The second is taking the time to uncover the root causes of what creates that love.

If you want to be sure your team members love your company, ask them to describe what it would take for that to be true (unless of course it already is!).

Use this same technique for your customers. Ask them what would it take for them to say that they love your product or service. Their answers will provide a road map for you to follow.

Reality Check

While many people claim they are working to create a great company, in reality it is not common practice. Why? Because not every leader has the courage, the passion and the perseverance it takes to create greatness. It takes a great deal of faith and steadiness to follow this love path.

What follows are a few examples of successful companies who have adopted a loving approach and have gained the loyalty of their customers to help you bolster your confidence.

Subaru: The Love Promise

How do Subaru owners feel about their cars? They LOVE them! How do we know? Because Subaru asked them.

It just so happened that the current Vice President of Marketing for Subaru of America was an MBA student of Tara's at Rutgers University. Tara was struck by the use of the word "love" in Subaru's ad campaigns, so she asked him about it. He said that the company had surveyed their customers and the number one message that came back loud and clear was that their car owners LOVED their Subarus.

So Subaru decided to build a marketing campaign around that message. You may recognize the tag line: *"Love: It's what makes a Subaru a Subaru."*

The campaign is part of a much larger endeavor run by Subaru called the Subaru Love Promise. According to Subaru, the Subaru Love Promise is *"A pledge to do right by the communities in which we all live and work."*

The love campaign launched in 2008 and in the five years that followed, Subaru's sales doubled in the U.S.

This is an amazing story that underscores the effectiveness of our suggested Appreciative Inquiry approach. First, Subaru went out and asked their customers how they felt about their cars. In this case, they discovered their customers already loved their Subarus. Then, Subaru was wise enough to build a whole advertising campaign based on love. That took some guts. But here comes the clincher. The whole point of Appreciative Inquiry is to be able to grow what you want to grow. By focusing on love, Subaru grew more love. Twice as much. Their sales doubled. Love, it turns out, is very powerful indeed.

We thought you would enjoy seeing the actual Love Promise. Great job Subaru!

The Love Promise

"The Love Promise is a promise to do right by our community by partnering with non-profit education, health, community, environment, and animal organizations to set Subaru apart through our deeds and the deeds of our partners. To be unlike any other car company by doing what is right and good, just for the sake of doing it."

We LOVE Wawa

Wawa is an awesome store. We love it and so do a whole lot of people in Pennsylvania, New Jersey and now Florida. With more than 600 stores, Wawa has been ranked the best convenience store in America for two years running. When we were facilitating our *Loyal, Loving Fans for Life!*™ workshop, we asked the room full of people, *"What is something that you love?"* One of the participants, Rich, who travels a lot, raved about Wawa. When he returns from a trip, he always stops into a Wawa because it makes him feel like he is "home." He is not alone. If you ask Wawa customers, they will tell you that *"We LOVE Wawa"* -- and that loyalty is fierce.

Wanting to learn more about the magic behind this brand, we took our Sounding Board™ CEO group to visit Wawa's home office. Speaking with one of their senior executives, we discovered their uncompromising commitment to their six core values – the first being "Value People". One way they value their people is with their Employee Stock Ownership Plan (ESOP). This program has worked so well that it has created numerous millionaires from team members who have become "owners."

The love that Wawa demonstrates for its team members ripples out into the culture of the store. If you ever shop at a Wawa, you will notice an amazing thing. Customers go out of their way to hold the door open for one another. It is wonderful to witness and it happens at every Wawa. We asked the leadership of Wawa if they were aware of this phenomenon. They were. They think it's because of their values. Just like when the Phanatic stops by to lovingly mess with a fan during a game, it is difficult for that fan to be grouchy or unkind after that encounter. Being loving inspires others to be loving in return.

Wegmans Rocks

Tom: Evan, not only do we share a love for the Phillies, classic rock, Dr. J and Wawa, but we also share a love for Wegmans. In fact, when Wegmans came to our town, I was one of the first in line when it opened.

Evan: Ha! We are on the same page, Tom! We did the same thing when our Wegmans opened. It was 6:00 am and we packed our family into the car. The kids thought it was crazy that we woke them up so early but there was an excitement in the air. No, we weren't going to Disneyworld. We were going to an opening…the opening of a supermarket. Yes, a supermarket. We thought we'd be one of the few crazies to be there. We were wrong. Very wrong. When we pulled into the parking lot we saw a huge line of people waiting to get in. It was like when crowds camp out all night long to get tickets to a great concert.

The folks who run Wegmans weren't surprised. They were prepared. They were prepared because it happens every time they open a new store. Who would have thought a supermarket could attain superstar status?

This year, 2016, Wegmans, a family-owned company, ranked #4 on the Fortune 100 Best Places to Work List. It's the 19th, yes the 19th consecutive year they have made the top 100 list. Is there any coincidence that consistently being one of the top ranked, best places to work makes them one of the most attractive places to shop? It's clearly part of their strategy; Wegmans knows that when their people feel respected and well-taken care of, they will pass that respect and love on to their customers.

Recently, we were hosting an executive retreat and talking about the allure of Wegmans. There were no women in the room and as we talked, each of the men in the group had a confession. They loved shopping at Wegmans. It was laughable as they each shyly admitted that fact. They liked Wegmans so much that they actually looked for excuses to go. On the surface, they couldn't put their finger on why. Was it the service, the way the store is laid out or the wide range of products? Yes, yes, and yes. The place is simply excellent.

That excellence, we contend, is the result of the power of love in action. Love can make people do things with fervor that ordinarily they don't want to do at all. One of the great benefits of creating world-class cultures is that it taps into people's discretionary energy. People will be inspired to go beyond doing that which is required of them. Not only will they do more, they will do it with passion. Doesn't every leader want to surround themselves with people purposely going above and beyond the call of duty?

When I'm shopping at Wegmans, I often notice how well-dressed the team members are and how neatly the shelves are stocked. One day, as I was checking out, I asked the cashier why everyone's uniforms are always neat and clean. To him, I am just another shopper in shorts and flip flops, not a student of leadership, but his response was as if he was talking to Mr. Wegman. He answered without hesitation, *"It's our values. It would be inconsistent with our values if I came to work any other way."* Love produces excellence. Wegmans does an amazing job of loving their people, their customers, and their company. Are you starting to see how nothing trumps love?

PART 2

HOW
to LOVE

CHAPTER 5
ONE LOVE *doesn't* FIT ALL

Tom: Evan, I have a confession to make.

Evan: What's that, Tom?

Tom: Not everybody loves the Phanatic.

Evan: WHAT? Say it isn't so.

Tom: It's true. My guess is that you didn't talk to Tommy Lasorda before you started to write this book.

Evan: You're right. I never did.

Tom: Well, it's probably a good thing you didn't talk to him. The former Los Angeles Dodgers manager wasn't a big fan of my friend, the Phanatic. When Tommy was still managing, the Phanatic would dress a dummy in a Tommy Lasorda jersey and throw it around the field in front of the visitor's dugout. Tommy would pace back and forth, kick, scream, and throw baseballs at the Phanatic's noggin. One day, he marched out onto the field, grabbed the dummy, whacked the Phanatic over the head with it and stormed back into the dugout. Of course, the fans loved it! The feud raged on for years. The Phanatic would always have something up his sleeve when Tommy and the Dodgers came to town. Even though Tommy wore the Dodger blue, his face would turn Phillies red whenever the Phanatic appeared.

Evan: OK, so one guy doesn't like the Phanatic. Big deal.

Tom: There's also that first base umpire in Harrisburg.

Evan: Uh-oh. What happened?

Tom: When I want to go for the really big laughs, I put a dress on the Phanatic and convert him from the Phillie Phanatic to Phyllis Phanatic. It's can't miss comedy! One night, I was performing at a minor league game in Harrisburg and rode out onto the field to dance to Mariah Carey's song "Hero". I saw the ump, jumped off the bike and slow danced around him. When I tweaked his backside with a well-placed "goose," the guy ejected the Phanatic from the game! Hard to believe, but I found the only umpire in baseball without a sense of humor.

Evan: OK, two guys aren't big fans.

Tom: Now that I think about it, the entire state of New York probably won't be inviting the Phanatic over for Thanksgiving dinner anytime soon either. The Phanatic has been smashing New York Mets helmets for over 30 years. The routine is always the same. When the Mets come to town, a tuxedo-clad Phanatic rides out onto the field between innings carrying a Mets helmet. With Frank Sinatra crooning "New York, New York" over the loud speakers, the Phanatic waits for the line, "these little town blues" and proceeds to smash the helmet with a heavy tamper. The crowd goes nuts every time.

The 2013 All Star Game was held at Citi Field in Queens and, as usual, all of the major league mascots were invited to attend the weeklong festivities. Every year, the mascots work the events around the game including the Home Run Derby. Before the Derby begins, the mascots are introduced to the crowd. When it was announced that the All Star Game would be in New York that year, I prepared myself for the reaction the Phanatic was going to get. The Mets fans did not disappoint. When the Phanatic was announced to the sellout crowd, the boos were so deafening, people in the Bronx could hear it! A funny thing happened that night with those New York fans. When I was in costume and greeting fans as they entered the ballpark, the reaction was the same from the die-hard Mets fans. They would call out, *"Yo, Phanatic, you suck! Now come over here for a photo. I gotta' show my friends I met you!"* So I'm here to say that beneath all the boos, Mets fans really love the Phanatic!

Evan: So it sounds like just about everybody loves the Phanatic! Your story is a great example of the point we want to make. One love doesn't fit all. I have a great example of this myself.

The popular on-line shoe company Zappos has an amazing policy for new hires. They will pay you $2,000 not to take the job. You've got that right - $2,000 not to take the job. As team members go through the training process there comes a jumping off point. You have two options: do you want to continue, or do you want to leave? It's a choice you get to make. Their tag line is "Delivering Happiness". I am a loyal loving customer and they have delivered happiness to me on a consistent basis. In order to create and protect this amazing culture, they are very careful about who they hire. They need folks who love their culture as much as they do. It's so important to them that it is worth paying $2,000 to have you opt out. They know that the cost of having people on their team who are not loyal loving fans is much more expensive than $2,000. As amazing as their culture is, it is not for everyone.

Lots of people love the Phanatic, but he's not everyone's cup of tea. We just found out that Tommy Lasorda, most of New York City and at least one ump in Harrisburg Pennsylvania are not big fans. We're sure there are many others. One love does not fit all. What is loving to one person may be a turn off to another. You may love a particular restaurant but your friend doesn't care for it. Does that mean the place isn't exuding love principles? Absolutely not. The point is that we have to love full out and create our own special formula for love. We need to define organizational cultures that embrace a particular brand of love. In doing so, we will attract a cadre of employees and customers who share that unique version of love. At the same time, we need to be cognizant of whom we invite into our world. We need leaders and staff who will buy in, protect, uphold and love our version of love.

Not everyone can step into the Phanatic's costume and pull off his brand of magic. Who is leading your organization? Who is serving your customers? Who is representing you? Are they exuding your special and unique form of love?

Clearly, one love doesn't fit all, but what do we do with that awareness? How can this knowledge help us to more fully unleash the untapped potential of people and organizations? We cannot expect everyone to get it. Our corporate culture may not be the right fit for everyone. It also means we can't be dogmatic. What works for you may not work for another. How do we become more flexible so that we can unleash more love in others?

In his wonderful book, *The Five Love Languages*, author Gary Chapman explains this so well. He demonstrates that each of us has our own love language. We show and feel love in different ways. What feels loving to one person may not be to another. We have to learn what their love language is and speak it to them in a way they will understand.

How can we effectively communicate to those we lead and how can we show appreciation in ways that will be well received by others? An obvious way is to ask those around you about their preferences. What is their preferred way of being loved, cared for and motivated? Understand that the simple act of asking them is a loving gesture.

While we know it's smart to customize your leadership approach to adapt to the preferred styles of your team members, it's also important to stand firm on your standards and never lower the bar. As leaders, while we need to create environments that welcome all types of people, we must remain true to the core values of the organization. We can remain firm on the value, yet flexible in the delivery.

Tom: So the cat's out of the bag. Not everyone loves the Phanatic, but since everyone's love language is different, I have to custom fit the Phanatic's love for others. There are baseball purists out there who think big video screens, music between innings and mascots don't belong in the game. For those fans, only a bat, ball and glove are required and all the other things are just a distraction. That's OK, but it does present me with a challenge when I'm roaming the stands and looking to play around with someone. If there is a guy sitting behind home plate keeping score in his program and not showing any interest in the Phanatic's antics, I pass right by. On the other hand, if there is a guy sitting behind the dugout wearing a Mets jersey and playfully taunting the Phanatic, he gets a shirt over the head or a lap full of spilled popcorn.

Evan: You make a good point, Tom. We are a big fan of the Myers-Briggs Type Indicator. Along with DISC and other personality assessments, organizations can become aware of the many different styles each of us have for making decisions, utilizing our time, and getting along with others. The best leaders learn how to adjust their interactions to align with the individual preferences and styles of the people they work with. In many ways, this is the mastery of leadership. Most people can do the tasks of their job quite well, but the differentiator is our ability to manage our relationships. The great Henry Ford said: *"Why is it that every time I hire a pair of hands, I get a whole person with them?"* He was alluding to the magnitude and importance of learning how to deal with a broad array of personalities. The same goes for being loving to the people we lead and to our customers. How do we love people in a way that matches their style and their preferences?

Tom: The Phillie Phanatic not only delivers individual styles of love to the fans in the stands, he has a lot different personalities that he juggles on the field as well. Most players who come to town enjoy messing around with the Phanatic before the game. It is a long season for them but it is still a game so why not have some fun? Players will throw bubble gum, packs of sunflower seeds and water cups while the Phanatic taunts them in front of the dugout. I've been hit by shaving cream pies and have been attacked by players who bring their own super soakers to the game.

One way the players taunt the Phanatic is by stealing the key to his ATV. This gag never gets old. A player will sneak up to the 4-wheeler while I'm not looking, grab the key and run back to the dugout. When the Phanatic returns to his vehicle and notices the keys missing, a frantic search ensues. When the Phanatic looks into the dugout, players point to one another as if to say, *"It wasn't me, it was him!"*

Eventually, the player will stand at the top of the dugout and dangle the key for the Phanatic to see.

Now comes the fun part – trying to get the key back. Detroit slugger Miguel Cabrera didn't wait for me to broker a deal with him to get it back. He snatched the key out of the ignition and then threw it to a fan sitting behind the dugout. The Phanatic pointed to the fan in the stands and gestured for Cabrera to get the key back. Since neither the Phanatic or I speak Spanish, it's unclear what Cabrera said, but I think it was along the lines of, *"You're on your own, amigo."*

The late Jose Fernandez, the starting pitcher for the Miami Marlins, was known to mix it up with the Phanatic before the game. On one occasion, he stole the key and refused to give it back. In the Phanatic's mind, the act of stealing his key is a felony and any perpetrator should be prosecuted to the fullest extent of the law. I walked over to a police officer, who was standing on the field nearby, and demanded he do something to Fernandez. He offered me his handcuffs and let the Phanatic make the arrest. With hands behind his back, the Phanatic led Fernandez into the dugout. Sadly, the arrest didn't stick because the Phanatic can't talk and couldn't read the pitcher his rights.

Normally, to get the key back, I will swallow my pride (and the Phanatic's), and drop to my knees and beg. The Phillie Phanatic is a proud bird so watching him humiliate himself by begging for the key is not a pretty sight. Sometimes I will sit up on my knees and beg like a dog pleading for a Milkbone. The player will motion to the Phanatic to roll over, sit up and roll over again.

Some players make me kiss their feet in order to get the key back. By this time, all the Phanatic's pride has gone out the window but with the ATV on the field, and the game about to begin, I will do anything to not delay the start of the game.

The Atlanta Braves take the stolen key game a step further. After they steal the key, they make the Phanatic do the infamous Tomahawk Chop to get it back. For those readers not aware, the Tomahawk Chop is a time-honored tradition in Atlanta where the Braves fans lift and drop their arm like an axe to salute their hometown team. This poses a serious dilemma for the Phanatic. He has to get the key back, while saving face with the Philly crowd. So in a bid for some sort of divine intervention, I drop to my knees in prayer and look up to the heavens, pretending to ask the 'big man' if I can do the Tomahawk Chop just this once in exchange for the key. Satisfied that things are square with Him, I turn my attention back to the Braves players and attempt to do one chop. The Phanatic struggles mightily and uses his other arm to push down the offending arm. When the Phanatic finally does the Chop, the players high-five each other and give back the key. As the Phanatic walks away from the dugout, I pretend to be struck by lightning, shaking uncontrollably and then collapsing to the ground.

Clearly, the 'big man' is not a Braves fan.

Messing around with the players before the game is a big part of the Phanatic's act from night-to-night. The crowd loves it and I feel like I'm at my best when the pros are having fun and playing with the Phanatic. Before every game, players warm up on the field, playing catch and stretching. Often, the Phanatic will join the players in their pre-game rituals. Calisthenics for the Phanatic means trying to touch his toes without falling and rolling his belly from side to side. One day, Toronto outfielder, Jose Bautista, challenged the Phanatic to keep up with his exercise regime. Bautista squatted and bullfrog-hopped across the field. The Phanatic tried to keep up but looked more like a green sumo wrestler slogging through quicksand. Next, the playful outfielder did a handstand, drawing cheers from the crowd. Not to be out done, the Phanatic countered with a set of one-armed pushups. When Bautista attempted his push-up, he crumbled to the ground, conceding victory to the Phanatic.

Most players love the Phanatic and when they fool around with me it can be a lot of fun. However, love is a two-way street. Not every player wants to mix it up with the Phanatic.

There are players who don't want to get involved in the pre-game shenanigans. The San Diego Padres have always been a team that likes to have fun with the Phanatic. Tony Gwynn was not one of those players. The late, great Padres outfielder was one of the most focused players to come to town. He never said a bad word to me while I was out there messing with his teammates, but he never acknowledged me either. Tony would do his stretching exercises, prepare for the game and never look at the Phanatic. That type of focus is one of the reasons Tony landed in the Hall of Fame. Thankfully for the Phanatic, not all players approach the game with the same type of focus. When I encounter a player that has their game face on, I just move on to the next player who looks like they may want to have some fun.

Evan: Great stories, Tom. Now how can we use these examples outside of the ballpark? What can you do if your organization is not a match for your style? It doesn't mean you have to leave. You can look for ways to be true to you.

I taught in an MBA program for almost a decade. I had a student who worked for a large military contractor whose work was very technical. After working there for a short period of time, she realized that the culture was not a fit for her in many ways. She was a very outgoing, dynamic and expressive person. She loved talking and dealing with others. She noticed that many of her co-workers avoided personal interaction and chose to send emails, even if the recipient of the email was sitting one desk over. People did not get up and talk to each other. She was almost in tears in class as she realized that her work environment was so contrary to her way of being. She was upset because she thought that she had to leave and go elsewhere. The next time the class met, she arrived with a smile. She explained that she was still upset at work the next day but then it dawned on her. She loved talking to people – she felt that this was when she did her best work. She realized that she could get up from her desk and go talk to people rather than hide behind her emails. Nothing was stopping her, so she just did it. It made her day and maybe it made theirs, too. Even though her work environment was not an exact match for her, she realized that she could improve it.

At times we may find ourselves in environments that are not a match for our style but that doesn't always mean we need to leave. We can look for ways to bring our own version of Phanatic love to the situation we are in right now.

Imperfect Love

We will never get love right 100% of the time. None of us will. We will all fall short of always being loving. There will be times when we are unkind, impatient, and harsh. We like the phrase, "strive to" – strive to become loving in all our business dealings; Strive to become more loving in our interactions; Strive to become more like the Phillie Phanatic. Sometimes, however, even the Phanatic gets it wrong.

Tom: We all strive to be the best we can be. We all try to be excellent, to be caring and loving. And the Phillie Phanatic always tries to be funny. Making the fans laugh is a big part of the love equation for the Phanatic, but sometimes he comes up short.

We had a Seventies promotion one night and I decided to dress the Phanatic up as Greg Brady, the oldest son in *The Brady Bunch*. Looking nothing like Greg Brady, between innings the Phanatic danced to the Brady's hit "Sunshine Day" wearing a black wig, bell bottom pants and a flowered shirt. There was no laughter and no applause. In fact, I can still hear the cricket-chirping sound in my head.

The Phanatic used to perform at a celebrity softball game every year in Puerto Rico. On our first trip to San Juan, the Phanatic was excited to mix in with the locals and show that he knew their culture. But the problem is that the Phanatic is geographically challenged and does not have a firm grasp of places other than Philadelphia and the Galapagos Islands. So the Puerto Rican fans were a little miffed when the Phanatic came out between innings dressed in a poncho and sombrero to do the Mexican Hat Dance.

Sometimes, it's all about timing. It is much easier to get laughs when the home team is winning but when they're not, the crickets return. In 2007, the Phillies made the playoffs for the first time in 14 years. The city was fired up as we prepared to face the Colorado Rockies in the first round of playoffs. It was a big game so I made sure I had my secret weapon ready to go for the 5th inning routine – Matt Mehler. Matt is one of my back-up Phanatics (I have three) and makes community appearances in costume throughout the year. Matt was born to entertain and is the Phanatic's foil and straight man for skits on the field and on the dugout. For Game One of the playoff series, Matt came up with one of his crazy characters – Johnny Mountain. Legend has it, Johnny was born in the backwoods of the Colorado Rockies and idolized John Denver. He wore a big cowboy hat, chaps and a brown leather vest with fringes on his sleeves. I planned to run Matt out to the third base coach's box, dressed in his ridiculous Johnny Mountain outfit, and playfully abuse him as he sang John Denver's hit, "Rocky Mountain High." The game started and the Phillies quickly found themselves down 3-0. All of the excitement was drained out of the ballpark by the time the 5th inning rolled around. People were not happy that the Phils had come out of the gate flatter than a pancake. The key to comedy is timing, and I knew the timing was terrible as I rode onto the field for the skit.

Our long-time PA announcer, Dan Baker, introduced our special guest.

"Ladies and gentlemen, please give a warm Philadelphia welcome to Colorado Rockies fan and legendary recording artist – Johnny Mountain!"

The fans response: *"Boooooooooo!"*

Johnny started to sing and the boos got louder. The first thing the Phanatic did was break Johnny's guitar in half, ala John Belushi in the movie, *Animal House*. Maybe the fans never saw the movie and didn't get the reference to that particular scene because there wasn't much of a response from the crowd. Johnny kept on singing as I lined him up and shoved a shaving cream pie in his face. Despite the distractions, Johnny plugged away and never stopped singing. Before leaving the field, I de-pants Johnny leaving him standing there in his boxers with shaving cream dripping down his face. Normally, this would have been a routine that killed but because the team was losing the biggest game of the year, it only got a few laughs.

It was tempting to hold back because the situation was tense. Maybe I should have played it safe and shot some free t-shirts into the crowd -- that would have been a guaranteed win. But instead, I decided to go for the big laugh. At times, being loving takes courage. I knew not everyone was going to love my act, but that wasn't a good enough reason for me to stop. I had to be true to myself and the spirit of the Phanatic. Sometimes our love will be imperfect, but that's part of the game.

In your organization you will face similar circumstances that require a degree of courage, will you play it safe or swing for the fences?

CHAPTER 6
WHAT WOULD *the* PHANATIC DO?

Tom: So far, we have made the business case for love, began to define what love is and learned that love isn't one-size-fits-all. Now what?

For the Phanatic, that's easy. Hug, high-five, smooch and make people laugh. Go into the community to spread the joy, spread the love. Visit nursing homes, hospitals and schools. Dance, celebrate and have fun.

Chances are, you don't have a mascot costume hanging in your closet. If you do, dust it off, strap it on and go party! But if you don't own one, don't worry. This book isn't about teaching you how to be the actual Phillie Phanatic. It's about love, being aware of its presence, choosing how to act in a loving manner and making life more fulfilling for you and the people you touch every day.

The Phanatic is a great example of how one person (or bird, in this case) can generate such positive energy. When Evan and I were developing our love principles and looking at everyday situations we face in our own lives, we asked ourselves the question, *"What Would the Phanatic Do?"*

For a mascot like me, that is the mother of loaded questions. In many cases, the Phanatic might flirt with a pretty girl, shine a bald head or steal somebody's nachos, so you might not want to do *everything* the Phanatic does. Nevertheless, when you have the mindset of the Phillie Phanatic, good things happen. Actor Jack Nicholson attended a Phillies game a few years back. I found out he was at the game in the first inning and started to think like the Phanatic. *"What Would the Phanatic Do?"* Knowing that one of Jack's notorious roles was the Joker, I grabbed a Batman costume that was tailor-made for the Phanatic and cruised out onto the field between innings, while the theme song to Batman blared over the PA system. First, I flapped my bat wings around the third base coach, doing my best caped-crusader impersonation. At that point, Jack's face appeared on our video board, laughing at Bat Phanatic's antics. Our video guys did a split screen on the board with Jack on one side and Bat Phanatic on the other. Jack was wearing a New York Yankees cap so in the Phanatic's eyes, he was still a villain. I drove the ATV in front of his front row seats behind home plate and taunted Jack by slowly flapping my bat wings and shadow boxing in front of him. As the crowd roared, Jack knew that he had been beaten. The Phanatic's encounter with Jack that night played out just like it usually does in the comic strip. The Joker always looks like he has the edge but Batman always gets the last laugh.

Evan: I did it, too, Tom! I asked myself, *"What Would the Phanatic Do?"* and I'm telling you, it worked!

As I walked into Sacred Heart Elementary School in Camden New Jersey to lead our Dare to Dream™ program for a classroom of sixth graders, I asked myself, *"What is my purpose here?"* I realized that I was coming to share love and to be an ambassador of possibility. While I wasn't dressed in green feathers and wearing giant shoes, I realized that I could be the Phanatic. It was an exciting 'aha' moment.

The phrase, *"What would the Phanatic do?"* entered my mind. It was a delightful and exciting thought; it was a perspective-shifter. I could have gone and done my job and that would have been fine, but by asking myself, *"What would the Phanatic do?"*, I was connected to a bigger game which made me feel more confident and carbonated.

As I answered the question, I imagined the Phanatic having joyous interactions. He would be enthusiastic and contagiously optimistic. He would go for it, realizing that this was a special moment for these kids. He would give it his all.

I walked through the doors all "Phanatic-d up." I didn't have to change my clothes because the change I made was inside of me…making a decision to be upbeat and playful. That's a choice we all get to make.

When we choose to live out the Phanatic's purpose, we can go anywhere with this spirit of love – to an inner city school in Camden, a board room in Denver, a factory in Cheboygan or home through our own front doors.

It's important to customize your Phanatic-inspired approach to fit your style and the situation, to custom fit the Phanatic's mindset to yours. Ask yourself, *"What would my version of the Phanatic do?"* Ask, *"How can I be loving and caring in this situation?"*

This question works for organizations as well, just ask *"How can we unleash the full potential of our people?"* Ask, *"How can we love our customers from their perspective?"* Ask, *"How can our product or service make the world a better place?"*

As you read on, exactly how to do this will become clearer. You will better understand how to unleash the amazing power of love. Soon, you will be able to answer the question, *"What would my Phanatic do?"* with ease.

CHAPTER 7
THE DNA *of* LOVE™

To best answer the question, *"What would the Phanatic do?"* it helps to first understand what the Phillie Phanatic actually does. So, we spent some time examining that – sort of like watching game films and breaking down the exact motions of a pitcher. We put the Phanatic in slow motion and observed.

And our observations paid off. Like the great scientists Pasteur, Newton and Madame Curie, we had our breakthrough discovery. We discovered The DNA of Love™ – the genetic instructions for how to create love. How great is that? Two loveable idiots find themselves at the forefront of DNA research, breaking ground in the science of love. Could the Noble Peace Prize be far behind? Imagine our beloved giant green bird heading to Sweden to receive the ultimate recognition in scientific research!

"We hereby bestow this great honor on the Phillie Phanatic for discovering the DNA of Love."

As we analyzed the Phillie Phanatic's encounters, we realized there are three-steps to his loving approach – Decide Love, Notice Love, Act Love.

"Ladies and Gentlemen, the DNA of LOVE"

DECIDE LOVE

In reviewing the Phillie Phanatic's replay tapes, we realized that something very significant happened before he ever started his antics. The action is invisible to the naked eye, but it is a powerful part of his "secret sauce". Each time, before making a public appearance, the Phanatic makes a decision to be loving. This decision is his secret sauce because he uses it to inform all of his actions.

Every person or organization that has achieved any level of greatness got there by making a decision to be great. That is where greatness starts – with a decision.

In his best-selling book, *Good to Great*, author Jim Collins nails this one. His book is an exploration of what makes some companies great while others remain good. Like us, his research showed that greatness starts with a decision.

Every action we take is informed by a decision– consciously or unconsciously. When we intentionally decide to be more loving, we catapult our love quotient. Deciding to be loving is an accelerator of love. We are letting the universe and our deeper selves know what we care about. By deciding to be loving, we will naturally attract more love and we will become more loving.

Being loving is not a choice we make once. It's a decision we make over and over again. In every encounter, we have choices in how we can respond. If we don't make a conscious decision to act in a loving way, we run the risk of defaulting to random reactions.

When we become intentional about being loving, we will start seeing the amazing impact of this approach. Making a decision is how it all starts. Simply, ask yourself: *"How can I be loving in this encounter?"* Deciding to be loving is always the first step.

NOTICE LOVE

The Phanatic walks out and sees 40,000 fans in the stands. As he maneuvers his way through the crowd, he isn't just getting from point A to point B. He is on the hunt. He is looking for the right opportunity to spread some love. Twenty-eight years of performing as the Phanatic has given him great skill for sniffing these moments out. It is second nature to him now.

As leaders, we get to play the same game. There is an important step between the decision to love and taking actions of love. We first have to be tuned into the opportunities. If we are not paying attention, they can slip right past us.

So what do you look for? How do you notice?

There are four main areas to focus upon. The first is your people. The second is your customers. The third is your products and services. The fourth is your systems and processes.

Here are a few questions to get you started:

1. People: How do we make the onboarding experience more welcoming and effective? How can we ensure that everyone feels appreciated? Are we giving our people a chance to grow and develop?

2. Customers: What can we do to surprise and delight them? How can we make the service personal?

3. Products and Services: How can we make products of the highest quality? What are the little things that will make a big difference? How can we be best-in-class?

4. Systems and Processes: Where can we make our systems easier and more user friendly? How can we be more efficient? Do our policies allow everyone to do their best work?

There is another element in this Notice Love game - your gut. Like the Phanatic, over time you will develop a sixth sense. You will just know the opportunities. It can be an intuitive idea to improve customer service, a product improvement that hits you on the way to work, or a cool innovation to a work process.

Tracking things is also a form of noticing. Organizations track expenses, cash flow and retention rates. Why? Because noticing what is so allows us to make better decisions. Noticing is a form of knowledge.

The pure act of noticing is a power in itself and causes situations and people to change. If you've ever driven by one of those signs that display your driving speed, you know it makes you think about how you are driving.

Noticing is a two-pronged strategy. By actively noticing, we seek out and find more opportunities to exercise and increase love. Then by noticing the love that already exists, we increase it even more.

ACT LOVE

The Phanatic hones in on a fan. He knows exactly what to do and then, with confidence, he unleashes one of his many love antics. The key is taking decisive action. It's too easy to back away or worry if this is the right thing to do.

We all know how to be loving, it's not complicated. The main thing is to make the effort. It does not have to be perfect.

Still, you may wonder, where to start. To make this easier, we present the Four Levers of Love™.

Lever 1: Be Kind

One of the best ways to Act Love is to be kind. If we had to pick one overall criteria for love, being kind to one another would rank at the top of the list. We can't think of a greater accomplishment than to create a kind organization. Companies strive to hire the smartest and the most talented employees they can find, but if those people aren't being treated with respect and love, their talents will go to waste. If you want to achieve great customer service, being kind will never let you down. The act of being kind inspires loyalty. In his simplest and most profound form, the Phanatic is kind. When in doubt, be kind.

Lever 2: Be Excellent

One of the most loving things we can do for people is to create an environment where they are inspired to do their best work.

People want to do their best work. We perform best in an environment where those around us strive to do great work. We lead when we create world-class cultures, products and services. This is a great act of love because we are allowing others to raise their games to a higher level.

As leaders, the way to love your organization is to create systems and tools that are convenient and allow folks to do their best work. This is love in action.

Excellence applies to every area of our organizations: excellent people, excellent products, excellence processes and excellent profitably. If you want more love, strive for more excellence.

Acts of love are not always easy or fun. They can be downright hard, scary and challenging at times. Acts of love will call on us to make tough decisions. In our attempts to unleash the full potential of our organizations, we will sometimes do things that will anger certain people and bring negative reactions to us. Love is not for the faint of heart. Love takes courage. It requires us to be true to ourselves, which is not always easy to do.

Lever 3: Think Love

Thinking may not feel like an action but it is. Imagine that each thought we have is a seed that grows into a plant. Our lives are simply a garden of our thoughts. If you want to see what you are thinking, look at the quality of your life and you will see the sum total of your thoughts. If you want to change your life, or your organization, you have to begin by changing your thinking. The first step is to become aware of your self-talk. What thoughts do you have about yourself, your organization, your customers and the people you work with? Notice which thoughts are limiting and negative.

Evan: I was about to go to a meeting with a client. In the course of our business dealings with her, I wasn't happy with how she was treating us. Before the meeting, I talked to a colleague. He suggested that I clean up my negative thoughts about her before we started because my negative thoughts would create a negative energy. I closed my eyes and started to think about all of her positive qualities.

I certainly felt better about her, and our meeting went quite well.

If we want to create love, then it's important to think love. Here is an exercise that I have found to be quite useful. The next time you are with someone you have had disagreements with or feel anger towards, in your mind, start to tell them that you love them. You can say over and over again, *"I love you."*

If you are working on a project, tell yourself: *"This is a great project and it will turn out magnificently! We will all work together really well."*

Imagine the impact of this collective thinking on an organizational level.

It's important to imagine the positive outcome of all of our endeavors. We can use our thoughts to help create the reality we desire.

Our thinking has a tremendous impact on the quality of our lives. If you want to create more love, think more love.

Lever 4: Speak Love

This love lever is really simple and easy to use. What are you saying? Are you speaking words of love?

Do some research. Walk around your organization and listen. What is the language you are hearing? Are people complaining? Do you hear words of encouragement and enthusiasm? The language you hear will be a clear indicator of the level of love and excellence in your organization. It is a great litmus test. Take the time to listen to yourself. What is your language? Are you complaining, argumentative and correcting? Be honest with yourself and with your organization. Is your language upbeat, encouraging, positive and loving? It may sound odd, but one of the best ways to change your organization is to change your language. If you want to reinforce certain behaviors or attitudes, use language to do so.

Words are free, easy to change and they come out of our mouths all day long. This makes them a very valuable tool for creating more love.

PHEEL THE LOVE!

We see the amazing love people of all ages feel for the Phanatic. It blows us all away. By Deciding Love, Noticing Love and Acting Love you put yourself in the position to create loyal loving fans for life – just like the Phanatic has. This love and loyalty is the greatest thing because while other companies can match your products and your prices – it's really hard to replicate deep-seated loyalty.

How ironic -- being loving turns out to be your best competitive weapon.

PART 3

THE PRINCIPLES *of* LOVE

When we started to analyze the secret behind the Phillie Phanatic's amazing love, we stumbled upon core ingredients. We called them principles. We realize that these principles were universal - they didn't just apply to the Phillie Phanatic. They became the foundation of our *Loyal, Loving Fans for Life!*™ program and the jumping-off point for this book.

The Seven Principles not only feature memorable Phillie Phanatic stories, but they also serve as powerful examples to pave the way towards love. They will help you see exactly how the Phillie Phanatic generates such powerful love and loyalty. We will explain each principle and provide business examples that correlate. We will also illuminate the DNA (Decide Love, Notice Love, Act Love) inherent in each principle.

Our intention is to help you start to reap the benefits being loving brings.

Are you ready to start *Pheeling the Love?*

CHAPTER 8: PRINCIPLE #1

THE *big* SMOOCH!:
LOVE *them* FIRST

Tom: It's a bright sunny day at Citizens Bank Park. It's the bottom of the third inning, the Phillies are winning and people are happy. The Phanatic is doing what he always does at Phillies games – wreaking havoc. He's in the seats, spilling popcorn, sitting on laps, stealing purses, kissing babies, posing for pictures and smooching anyone wearing Phillies gear. I love my job!

A voice calls out from the crowd – *"Yo, Phanatic! Show me some love!"* I turn and see a guy standing in the middle of the aisle, arms stretched out and ready to give the Phanatic a great, big hug. Quickly, I size the guy up. He's a 20-something year old male, looking like he just stepped off the set of *Animal House*. His hands are free (surprisingly, he's not holding a beer), and his arms are outstretched. His shirt is untucked, the bottom of his belly protruding slightly over his belt. He has a big smile on his face. Perfect.

I move in for the kill. As we close in to hug, I quickly go for the bottom of his untucked shirt, grab it with both hands and in one swift motion, whip the shirt over his head. Frat Guy, as I now think of him, is now standing in the middle of the aisle, sans shirt, and still smiling. I wad the shirt into a ball and throw it into the next section of seats. He laughs, we hug and another memory is made. The Phanatic delivered on the guy's request, he showed him the love!

Evan: Ha! I LOVE it, Tom. That story sums up why the Phanatic is so well loved. It's because he loves you first. It's a universal truth – if you want people to love you, you have to love them first. In business parlance, if you want people to love your company, product or service, you have to love them first.

Tom: The "Big Smooch" is the Phanatic's way of loving you first. He dishes out the love, kisses and high-fives everywhere he goes. I'm pretty sure that if the folks at Guinness Book of World Records had been following the Phanatic around since his debut in 1978, he would rank at the top of the list for "Most High-Fives in a Lifetime". And remember, Evan, the Phanatic can't talk so he's generated all of this love and good will without ever speaking a word.

Evan: Sometimes you can say a lot without ever saying a thing. The high-five, the signature Phanatic kiss and his furry (sometimes smelly) bear hug is what we like to call the Phanatic's "Outward Expression of Optimism" (OEO). Just about everything the Phanatic does is an outward expression of optimism, except of course when the Mets are in town!

Tom: Well, I guess when the Phanatic smashes a Mets helmet on the field, it's an outward expression of optimism for Phillies fans, not Mets fans! One thing I love to do is spot a random fan about 20 feet away, lock eyes with that person, and then make an all-out sprint through the crowd to plant a giant kiss on his (or her) head. It's like we are long lost friends that haven't seen each other in years. The fan's reaction is always the same. He laughs and blushes and when the dust settles he gets that look on his face that says, *"I can't believe he picked me!"*

Evan: And that's exactly how it works in business. That is the feeling you want your customers and employees to feel every day. You want them to feel that they really matter. One of my favorite places to shop is Trader Joe's. I love the store for many reasons, but one of the biggest is because their crew members are so friendly. Trader Joe's consistently practices "The Big Smooch!" They make their customers feel special and loved. They do this by loving their crew members first. For example, before the Affordable Health Care Act began offering people affordable health care options, Trader Joe's offered their part-time employees health insurance. Typically, part-time employees are not offered health care coverage. It was one very important way the company loved their crew members.

Everyone wants to be appreciated, to feel special and feel like they matter. When you feel loved and appreciated, you can more easily love others.

Tom: I can relate to that, Evan. Working for the Phillies organization is like spending time with family. It can be a lot of fun working for a professional sports team, but the days and nights can be long. I spend more time with my fellow co-workers than I do with my family. Thank goodness we like each other! That atmosphere of love happens naturally at the Phillies. Take our lunch break, for example. We have a cafeteria-style lunch every day. The best part about it is that we all sit together, and that includes everyone from the president of the Phillies to the many interns that work for us. We talk about our lives, families and work. It's a great way to get to know everyone and it fosters that feeling of belonging.

Evan: That's good stuff, Tom. Feeling appreciated at work and loving your job and the people you work with is a gift. It's only when we feel special and loved that we can release that love for our customers, clients and everyone we meet. When we are in the love zone, our outward expression of optimism radiates from us. It's present at work, home and everywhere we go. In fact, EVERYTHING you do should be an outward expression of optimism.

Tom: OK, Evan, I just want you to remember that the next time you see the Phanatic at the game and he spills popcorn all over you, sits on your lap or sneezes on your cheesesteak, it just means that he cares!

How can the Phanatic make this kind of impact with a simple smooch or high-five? The answer is simple: people want to feel special and loved.

As we started to explore what creates love, this became our most critical and obvious principle. If we want our clients, our vendors and employees to love us, then we need to genuinely love them first.

Most likely, you won't be running around in a green costume high-fiving people, but there are principles at play here that apply to every person, every business and every situation. By the way, if you are inspired to run around your organization high-fiving folks, have a ball doing it.

One of the key ingredients to Loving Them First is consistency over time. Your organization must be committed to consistently delivering the love, over and over again. A simple example of a 'love habit' is responding to people's calls or requests promptly. It's an easy concept but one that yields positive results. Not only do people feel respected because you responded in a timely manner, but when we communicate with people they feel our intention. When we care about others' concerns, when we look out for their best interests, and go out of our way to help them, they experience the elements that create love. They feel special, noticed and well taken care of. The love comes when we consistently behave in this kind of manner. The love really grows when our actions and our intentions of care are genuine. That is what creates the momentum in other people's hearts. They experience our genuine caring acts over and over again, which steadily builds an experience of love. You can be blown away by an experience of care once, or a customer service call that went great. That can be an intense singular experience, but it turns into a love experience when it is repeated or experienced over and over again. Your goal should always be to have people genuinely feel and say, *"I love that place, that product, that person."* It is consistently caring in genuine ways that creates the love.

The other key component of this principle is initiative. The Phanatic loves them first. This is not a quid-pro-quo endeavor. You get an even greater love reaction when the other party feels that you loved them first. You need to take the initiative. This is not about sitting back and waiting for others to love you and then deciding to care for them. This is about making a decision and taking a positive action first and always. Love them first. Love your kids first, your spouse first and your customers first. Take the actions of caring first and consistently, and this will produce the love. How much love we receive back from others is not the point. The point is for us to make the decision to be loving, to care genuinely, to do acts of loving kindness, to be excited to see people, to be grateful and to share our enthusiasm.

Now here is the tricky part. It's really hard to show the love if you aren't feeling it yourself. It can be hard to love them first if you find it harder and harder getting out of bed to go to work each morning. We should always be loving, even when we don't love what we do. But our feelings of real love will explode when we have a strong belief in our organization, our people and our products.

We see this all the time when we are out in the world. We experience people who love their companies and their products and we also experience the negative energy of people who don't feel that love. To be a world-class organization and to have world-class love, it's critical to have the kind of passion and enthusiasm we described earlier. Tom loves being the Phillie Phanatic but he also truly loves the Phillies, he loves sports and he loves being a fan. If you get to know Tom, you'll feel his enthusiasm.

We can all increase our love by investing ourselves in the things we love. It may be hard for you to find things you love in life. It is a journey to open our hearts and find those things we love. Many of us have wounds in our lives that have shut down our ability to love. It may be a journey for you, to re-discover the love. We truly hope this book reminds you how important and worthwhile it is to find, cultivate and develop love. One of the best ways to open up our love is to live this principle. We don't have to wait for others. We can love them first.

DNA of Love

Decide Love

Tom: The Frat Guy story is a perfect example of how I decide to love in each one of the Phanatic's encounters. I size up fans quickly when I'm in costume and want to share some love. I heard the Frat Guy yell out, *"Yo, Phanatic, show me some love."* He had his arms out wide and a smile on his face. In that moment I made a quick decision. I told myself, *"This is a great opportunity to show this guy* *and the crowd what the Phanatic is all about. Time to show him some love."*

The fact is, from Day 1, the Phanatic has led with love. I remember going to a game as a kid and running into the Phanatic on my way back to my seat. It was the first time I had come face to face with him, and since the Phanatic was one of my heroes, I froze in shock. We stood staring at each other for a few seconds and then he lunged at me, grabbed my head with both hands and smothered my face with his green feathery snout. When we stepped back, I surprised the Phanatic by giving him a taste of his own medicine. I pretended to spit out his kiss before he got a chance to spit out mine. That memory has stayed with me all these years and I get a kick knowing that each time I lay a smooch on one of our fans, I might be making a memory that will last a lifetime for them, too.

Evan: How can the Phanatic make this kind of impact with a simple smooch or high-five? The answer is simple: People want to feel special and loved.

As Tom mentioned, the Phanatic has loved them first since Day 1. It was the essence of the Phanatic's creation and his original purpose for existing. Love was built into his DNA, and thus infuses his being and everything he does with purpose. We want to see more organizations utilize this same principle – to make the choice to be loving right at the core of the business enterprise and make it their purpose for being. We don't want love to be just as an ancillary tactic but instead, we want this principle to be the foundation of every organization's mission and vision.

Love is much more powerful when it sits at the core of purpose. When Isadore "Issy" Sharp opened the Four Seasons, he did so with a simple premise, a premise that permeates everything they do: how they treat their customers, and how they treat each other. Love is evident in their level of service, their attention to detail, and through every interaction with their guests. For Issy, this was the Golden Rule. The Golden Rule was their purpose for being. The Golden Rule is a beautiful version of Love Them First. The hotel and its brand are expressions of the choice, in this case, to 'be' the Golden Rule.

The Phanatic embraces the same choice. Love Them First. It is a choice you, too, can make personally in your life each day. What is my real purpose for going to work today and every day? Is it to get stuff done? Is it to make money? Is it to move up in the organization? These are all good things, but if you choose to put love first in your purpose, then you are unleashing your full potential, the full potential of the organization and the full potential of the universal life force. All of the other stuff will come along for the ride and with much more power and influence when you choose to Love Them First.

Today at work, you may need to correct the behavior or attitude of another team member. Love does not mean avoiding conflict or lowering your high standards. The question is how do we do it in a loving way? You may be upset in a moment today. How do you react in a loving way? It can be very challenging, especially because you may not be feeling the love in the moment. You won't always get it right, no one does. The point is, the opportunity is there for you to choose love and to allow love to be your guiding force in that encounter. When we stop and choose to love them first, magical things can happen in our relationships. Love is not an avoidance tactic. It is a powerful strategy for achieving excellence in all of our encounters.

Ask yourself, where is the opportunity for love? Where is the opportunity to do our best work? Where is the opportunity for excellence? Where is our opportunity to be great?

Notice Love

Tom: In the costume, I'm constantly surveying the crowd. We have fans of all shapes and sizes. Some fans are there just to watch a baseball game – "the purist" – and others are there for the game, atmosphere, food, fun and all that comes with it. I can read the signs from someone who just wants to watch the game and isn't interested in dancing with a big, green Muppet. That's OK, I just move along. I'm always on the lookout for the people who want to have fun with the Phanatic. When the Frat Guy yelled, *"Yo, Phanatic, show me some love",* I took notice!

Look around you. Look around your organization. It will be easy to notice all of the many opportunities where you can be loving.

Look at yourself. There may be a time when you are about to open your mouth to correct someone's behavior. Stop. Ask yourself, *"Is there a way I can do this in a more loving way?"* Maybe you are on a sales call. Stop. Ask yourself, *"How can I be honest, genuine and caring toward this person, toward their needs, to the company they represent? How can I do my best to help them reach their fullest potential? How can I provide the help that they need?"*

Act Love

Tom: When I heard Frat Guy yell, I knew that I had to act on it. In my mind, I know that when I act on an invitation like that, I have the ability to make a memory that lasts a lifetime. That's powerful stuff. Love can't be transmitted until we act on it.

I've noticed Frat Guy in the aisle and now I'm going to act on it. Now I've got to think, how should I engage this guy? Does he want to 'play' with me? Is he familiar with the Phanatic's act? How much love can this guy handle? There is more sizing him up – I have a clear path to him, his shirt is untucked, his hands are free, he looks like a guy who has gone shirtless for laughs at some point in his life. It's a warm day so if it takes a while for the guy to get his shirt back, he won't get frostbite.

If the Phanatic could speak, he probably would have yelled, *"I love you, man!"*, or *"I love that Phillies shirt you are rockin'"* or *"Come here and give me a hug, bro!"* Instead, as the Phanatic, I conveyed those words with body language. I turned and did a double-take, acting like he had gotten the Phanatic's attention. The Phanatic pointed to the guy like he was a good friend, hustled up the four or five steps with his arms out wide, looking like he was going to give his friend a great big bear hug. At that moment, Frat Guy is hooked. His buddy, the Phanatic, has singled him out and is ready to show him the love. When his shirt comes off and is tossed into the next section, he's now laughing and will have a memory that he won't soon forget.

While you may not have Frat Guy running around your company, everyone is reaching out for love in their own way. What can you do to make them all feel special?

Pheel the Love!

I'm pretty sure that after his unforgettable encounter with the Phanatic, Frat Guy has become a fan of the Phanatic's for life. Back at the keg party that night and for weeks, months and years to come for that matter, when the topic of mascots comes up, Frat Guy will blurt out to all his friends, *"I LOVE THE PHANATIC!"*

Not only did that incident make Frat Guy a Phanatic fan for life, it probably cemented his love for the Phillies as well. The Phanatic is on the front lines with the fans. He's the one that fans can reach out and touch. If the Phillies are losing and the game is dragging, a fan can walk away with a better experience if they laughed at the Phanatic that night. For the Phillies, the Phanatic is the "pocket of love", the part of the organization that consistently exudes fun and goodwill, no matter what is happening on the field.

Evan and I meet at Whole Foods all the time. The store has a person working during the busy lunchtime hours who engages people in conversation and helps customers find the shortest check-out line. This employee directing traffic at the check-out counters is Whole Foods' "pocket of love". When someone walks out of Whole Foods thinking, *"Boy, that person was a real pleasure to be around and he really helped me out"*, that customer will likely come back again and again. It might also help to sway their decision to shop at Whole Foods vs. the Mom's Organic Market that just opened right across the street!

CHAPTER 9: PRINCIPLE #2

SEE THROUGH *your* CUSTOMER'S CAMERA: MAKE *every* ENCOUNTER COUNT

The Phanatic and all great organizations create widespread love one encounter at a time. Likewise, each of us has many opportunities to do the same thing every day. Just think about the number of personal encounters you have daily. Imagine how many total encounters your organization has in one day. The number is staggering, but so is the opportunity. It means that each of us has in our control countless opportunities to create the love. This is where the rubber meets the road – each encounter counts. Each one adds up to a sum and it's that sum that creates the love we are experiencing.

Through the Phanatic, we re-discovered how to make encounters count towards love. We learned to see through our customer's eyes. We know that this is age old wisdom: live by the Golden Rule and care for others.

When we think of the people we encounter each day, we should constantly be asking ourselves, *"What does this person need? What is of value to them?"* Rather than being self-focused, the key is being other-focused. What will make our customer happy? What will help them be more effective? How can I help my customers be more successful? Great organizations create products and services that care for their customer's needs, one encounter at a time.

As the leader or a member of an organization, being loving is a decision we make repeatedly with each encounter. How do we put our own agenda aside and decide to focus on other's needs? In their wonderful book, *The Go Givers*, authors Bob Burg and John David Mann refer to the concept of "enlightened self-interest." You may call it karma or the law of reciprocity. In a nutshell, the authors assert that the best way to have our own needs met is to care for the needs of others.

Evan: Tom, you have been performing as the Phanatic for close to 30 years. Has anything changed?

Tom: Not much about the job has changed since the Phanatic made his debut in 1978. He's out there on the field wreaking havoc before the game. He has fun with the fans in their seats, performs on the field after the 5th inning and dances the night away on the Phillies dugout at the end of the 7th inning.

The one thing that has changed is the number of pictures the Phanatic poses for at each game. Think about it. Not long ago, we lived in a world without digital cameras, smartphones and Facebook. The Phanatic could roam the concourse during a ten game home stand and not pose for a single picture. Now, on those nights when 40,000 people are in attendance, that usually means that there are 40,000 cameras in attendance. There are nights when I feel that all 40,000 cameras are focused on me. No matter where the Phanatic goes, fans want a picture. The times I'm being swarmed by fans are when I feel like the 5th Beatle. Of course, not everyone knows how to actually use their camera phones.

"How do you turn this thing on?"

"What button do I push?"

"Oops, it didn't come out right. Can I take another?"

If I had a dime for every time I heard a fan utter one of these phrases, I'd have enough money to own the Phillies.

Evan: So the Phanatic is a popular guy. That's a good thing, right?

Tom: Yes, it's a good thing, but sometimes things can get a little out of hand. Here's an example. I was performing at a Lehigh Valley Iron Pigs game a few years ago. The Iron Pigs are the Triple-A affiliate for the Phillies. I was goofing around with the fans behind the dugout when a foul ball came screaming into the seats, hitting the Phanatic in the neck. Now that wouldn't be such a big deal but the Phanatic's neck is my face! I went tumbling back onto a fan's lap. The first thing that went through my head, besides the ball, of course, was that I was still alive. The second thing that hit me, besides the ball, of course, is that I'm a mascot and I had better start acting like one. The crowd was in hysterics as I wandered around dazed and confused (not that it was much of an act). I staggered through the row of seats and to the aisle where the girl, who was supposed to be my bodyguard, was sitting. I whispered in her ear, *"I'm hurt, you have to get me out of here."* She immediately grabbed her walkie-talkie, called for EMT and then proceeded to lead me up the steps on our way back to the locker room.

When we got to the top step and onto the concourse, a crowd was waiting to get their high-five, big smooch and to take photos with the Phanatic. I did my best to accommodate everyone as I could feel my eye slowly swelling shut. Out of the corner of my good eye, I could see two guys from the emergency medical staff rushing my way. *"Ah, help at last,"* I thought to myself. But my hopes of getting quick medical attention were dashed when I noticed one of the guys pull out his cell phone camera to take a picture of his partner with the Phanatic. After they got their picture, the two guys skipped away like a couple of giddy school girls, thrilled that they now had a great photo to post on their Facebook page.

Evan: So is that what it means when people say love hurts?

Tom: What can I tell you, I bleed for my art. Don't get me wrong. I know how cool it is to grab the Phanatic and get a selfie, but when I'm being swarmed by a mob of people all trying to get a photo with the Phanatic, I sometimes forget the power of that one-on-one encounter. Sometimes the only thing on my mind is *"How am I going to make it out of this crowd alive?"* A big part of my job is being ready to go for my routines on the field and on the

98

dugout so stopping for dozens of photos on my way to where I have to be can be frustrating.

I remember one night a few years ago. I had injured my back and had to miss a game. My assistant, Matt, filled in for me that night. Even though I couldn't suit up, I wanted to be there for Matt who was getting his chance to perform at his first game. I followed him onto the concourse and watched him work his way through the crowd. I noticed three teenaged girls working up the courage to approach the Phanatic for a photo. They handed me the camera and I took their picture with the Phanatic. Matt Phanatic did what I would do and continued along on his way through the crowd, high-fiving, hugging and posing for photos. Since I was out of the costume, I had a chance to see the aftermath of what happens when the Phanatic stops and poses for a photo. The girls took back their camera and huddled around it to see how the photo came out. They laughed and giggled and ran to show their other friends the funny photo.

That outer body experience had a big impact on me. It helped to reinforce the idea that every time the Phanatic encounters someone, he can be making a memory that lasts a lifetime. For some, maybe it's their first Phillies game and first time meeting the Phanatic. Others tell me, *"Phanatic, I've been trying to get a picture with you for years!"* I've had fans walk up to the Phanatic and show me a photo as them as a baby. Their mission is to get a modern day version of the photo – a before and after shot.

Granted, not every photo will be passed on from generation to generation. Not every photo will be hung over the fireplace or buried with a love one.

But some will.

DNA of Love

Decide Love

Maybe it's a hot summer day and I'm sweating buckets. Maybe I've already posed for 300 photos and I'm looking to get back to my dressing room for a break and a chance to get a drink of water. Maybe the person trying to take my photo is grabbing the Phanatic's fur and won't let go. Despite those conditions, I try to remind myself that the magic of the Phanatic comes when fans can get a personal meet and greet or photo with the big green guy. I have to decide to put the fans first, stop and spread a little love and maybe make a memory that lasts a lifetime.

Every manager of people can relate to this story. We all have plenty of work to do ourselves but as leaders, other people require our time. What do you do when you get stopped in the hallway, or asked for help when you have things to get done yourself? It can take great personal discipline to put aside our own work and give someone the time they need. The love really comes when, you not only stop to help them, but do so in such a way that they feel special and that their issue really matters to you.

Notice Love

Whether I am at the ballpark or at an outside appearance, working my way through a crowd and noticing the different types of fans is a big part of the job. The Phanatic tries to make some type of contact with everyone. I might notice a family of four, decked out in Phillies gear, with kids clutching Phanatic dolls and dad holding his camera getting ready for a photo. If I have my blinders on and rush to go where I need to go, I might miss an opportunity to make a special moment for that family. Pay attention, look out purposefully for opportunities to make an encounter count. These moments will present themselves to you all day long.

We are suggesting that leaders purposefully be on the lookout for opportunities to be helpful. One level of service is to help others when they ask for our help. We can take the idea of service to a higher level when we proactively look for opportunities to care for others. We love the concept of managing by "walking around". Great leaders make a point of taking time to walk around the company, not to be noticed, but to notice others.

Act Love

I've decided to do my best to stop for as many fans as I can and take note of my surroundings. Now it's time to act! This is the fun part. There are all kinds of ways to approach a fan, but as we said before, one love doesn't fit all. I have to adjust the style of the

Phanatic's love to each individual, each situation. Some fans are shy and reluctant to approach the Phanatic. I may take that blushing fan by the hand and have her friend take the picture. The Phanatic will go belly-to-belly with a heavy guy or pregnant woman. I'll gently slow dance with an elderly woman, chest bump a college kid and smooch a screaming fan. My head is always on a swivel, looking for opportunities to create a magic moment.

Evan: This does not have to be complicated or expensive. Ask yourself, what do our customers need? For years I taught at the AT&T School of Business. I was teaching a leadership course and the topic was diversity. One woman in the course told us that until they hired people in wheel chairs, it never dawned on them to create pay-phones that were low to the ground. They had not looked at the situation through all of their customer's eyes.

Say hello, smile, ask someone how they are doing, perform a random nice act, send a thank you note, apologize for a mistake you made. Each encounter creates another opportunity to look through your customers "camera".

Pheel the Love!

It's remarkable that the Phanatic can make such a powerful impact by simply stopping to pose for a picture. To brighten one life each day is a blessing. When I think of the number of photos and the number of impressions the Phanatic makes every time he is out and about with the fans, it puts a smile on my face.

While you most likely won't walk around your organizations taking pictures all day, the principle holds strong. Imagine all of the opportunities you each have to touch people all day long. Every email, every conversation and every chance encounter gives us opportunities to care for others.

There is a pressure we all feel to get our work done each day. Our natural instinct is to block out everything and everyone to get our job done. The challenge is to fight that urge and understand that our real job is taking the time to be there for others. Our real job is to turn the camera around and put others in focus. Our real job is to ask ourselves, *"What do they need?"* It is a very powerful life decision that helps to make every encounter count.

CHAPTER 10: PRINCIPLE #3
DUCT TAPE & HOT DOGS: BE COMMITTED *to* OPERATIONAL EXCELLENCE

Evan: I've watched you in action and I've noticed that you have a lot of fun at your job.

Tom: Well, if you can't have fun dressed as a funny green bird…then this job is definitely not for you.

Evan: The other thing I've noticed is how committed you are to your job.

Tom: Committed? You think I should be committed?

Evan: No! You're crazy, but not THAT crazy. I'm talking about how hard you work to make the Phanatic one of the best mascots in sports. It doesn't just happen by accident, does it?

Tom: Actually, there are a lot of people involved behind the scenes that help to make the Phanatic the best he can be and to make sure our fans have fun every time they come to a Phillies game. Let me ask you a question. What is the greatest invention of all time?

Evan: Well, I'm a big fan of Eli Whitney's cotton gin. Of course, the light bulb was a pretty important invention.

Tom: You're way off. Mankind's greatest invention has got to be the Phillie Phanatic's Hot Dog Launcher!

Evan: That was going to be my next guess.

Tom: I bring up the Phanatic's Hot Dog Launcher as an example of what happens behind the scenes when we shoot hot dogs into the crowd. Let me explain.

The launcher made its debut on Opening Day in 1996 and the Phanatic's been shooting cooked hot dogs at Phillies games ever since. When the Phillies moved from the Vet to Citizens Bank Park, the launcher received an upgrade. What started in '96 as a handheld three-and-a-half foot converted potato launcher has become a six-foot fiberglass hot dog, powered by liquid nitrogen and capable of shooting a hot dog clear out of the ballpark.

Sounds simple, right? Actually, it is (let's face it, this ain't rocket science), but there is a lot that has to take place for a lucky fan to catch a free hot dog at a Phillies game. When the conditions are right for a night of hot dog launching, I phone Chris Long, our long-time entertainment director. She logs it into our in-game entertainment schedule, which sets off a series of events. Entertainment coordinator, Teresa Leyden, notifies our promotions team, who order the hot dogs from our ballpark concessionaire, Aramark. Members of our promotions team pick up the hot dogs and take them to the ground crew area on the service level to be prepared for flight.

How do you prepare a hot dog to be launched upwards of 300 feet? Good question. First, the hot dog is wrapped in aluminum foil to seal in the freshness. Next, the wrapped hot dog is rolled up into a piece of standard white computer paper and then sealed tightly with good old fashioned, run-of-the mill duct tape. If the hot dogs aren't wrapped the right way – KABOOM – you get an exploding hot dog and an angry head groundskeeper who has to clean it up. The promotions team mounts a bracket to the roll bar of a John Deere truck and the giant fiberglass hot dog is carefully locked into place. The nitrogen tank is hooked up and the regulator is cranked to 350psi. Two large hot dog signs are attached to either side of the truck, and voila, the Phillie Phanatic's Hot Dog Launcher is ready to rock. When the 5th inning ends, the large door leading to the field, swings open. Our sound man cues up *Who Let the Dogs Out,* or other hot dog launching music and before you know it, hot dogs are flying at Citizens Bank Park.

I only have a minute-and-a-half between innings, so I zip quickly to left field to shoot about five or six dogs. I make a turn towards the outfield where I shoot a few more over the outfield fence and finish up with another half a dozen flying franks on the right field side. If a hot dog falls a little short and ends up on the field, one of the members of our promotions team is there to scoop it up. Just before exiting the field, I'll shoot one up into the right field upper deck. If the wind is blowing right, the last dog will fly past the last row, over the brick façade and onto the street below. We drive off the field and back to the ground crew room, where the launcher is disassembled, packed away and stored until the next time we want to feed our fans Phillies franks.

Evan: Wow, it sounds like you have this hot dog shooting thing down to a science.

Tom: You need to strive for excellence, but sometimes things go wrong, even when it comes to shooting hot dogs. One day, before a Phillies game and before fans had entered the ballpark, we took the hot dog launcher out onto the field to shoot a television commercial. We shot dogs into the empty seats and at bulls-eye targets we had set up in the stands. Just for fun, we launched a few right out of the park. Later that day, I was back in my office when I noticed a commotion outside my door. One of my co-workers informed me that there was a bomb scare somewhere around the ballpark and that it was all over the news. I turned on the TV and sure enough, there was a TV reporter, reporting live at Citizens Bank Park, describing the scene:

"It seems as though three oblong packages, wrapped in duct tape, were found outside the First Base Gate. The ballpark will remain closed until the situation is resolved. The bomb squad is on the scene."

I'll admit, I'm not the sharpest knife in the drawer, but I did some quick calculations, put two and two together, and figured out what was happening.

"Wait a minute. Three oblong packages wrapped in duct tape? Those aren't bombs – they're hot dogs!"

I ran from my office to tell my boss to call off the dogs (quite literally, call off the dogs since the bomb sniffing dogs had arrived with the bomb squad) but it was too late. The bomb squad detonated the "suspicious packages" and the hot dogs were destroyed.

The moral to this story – strive for operational excellence but know, that at one point or another, you might bomb.

DNA of Love

Decide Love

The Phillie Phanatic is considered to be one of the best mascots in sports. The national sports shows talk glowingly of the Phanatic, he's been voted top mascot in dozens of on-line polls and when a visiting team comes to town, their announcers rave about the antics of the Phanatic. That level of popularity didn't happen by accident. The Phillies organization committed to the character from the day they envisioned a mascot for Philadelphia's baseball team.

The Phillies went to the very best in the business to create the costume. Bonnie Erickson was working for Sesame Street's Jim Henson when the Phillies called. She had created iconic characters like Miss Piggy and other Muppet characters. Then the Phillies turned to Dave Raymond to be the first man to step into the character's oversized green shoes and bring the Phanatic to life.

Dave was working part time in the promotions department the year the Phillies were getting ready to unleash the Phanatic for the first time. Dave was a good athlete and a punter on the University of Delaware's football team. Coincidently, the team was coached by his father, Tubby Raymond, who led the Blue Hens for 36 seasons and posted 300 wins. It turns out that Dave was the perfect man to breathe life into the Phanatic. He brilliantly brought the personality of a mischievous 10-year-old to the Phanatic and at the same time, gave him a heart of gold. He broke new ground by engaging players, coaches and umpires in the act, and quickly made the Phanatic an overnight success.

Having a great mascot costume and a gifted performer was a great way to help guarantee that the Phanatic would be a success from the start. But what really put the Phillie Phanatic on the map was the commitment of the Phillies organization to make the Phanatic the best in the business.

The Phillies have always invested in the "business" of the Phanatic. The big green guy has all the cool toys – a four-wheeler to drive on the field, a van to take to all the outside appearances, new outfits to dress in, t-shirt and hot dog launchers and all the Silly String and Super Soakers he needs. The Phillies have made sure that the Phanatic brand is omnipresent at the ballpark, with his image appearing everywhere on the concourse and souvenir stands. The Phanatic is often the focal point of many of the club's community outreach initiatives and has been a central figure in the organization's branding and advertising campaigns.

The point is, that the popularity the Phanatic has enjoyed since his debut did not happened by accident. It remains an organization-wide commitment to make the Phanatic the most entertaining mascot in sports. As we explore the concept of Decide Love, it is easy to see that in order to be excellent you need to decide that excellence is critical to your organization. We like the phrase, *"This is the way we do things around here."* Every great organization we have studied has made this decision - *"excellence is the way we do things around here."* It's non-negotiable. Until you make this decision, it will be impossible to create a truly great organization and one that people truly love.

Notice Love

Evan: One of the keys to building organizations that are operationally excellent is noticing where you are excellent and where there are gaps in your excellence. How do you consistently be on the look-out to improve?

As previously mentioned, I run a group called Sounding Board™. It's comprised of CEOs and c-suite leaders who sign on to get backstage tours of high-performing organizations. Our hope is that our members will leave these visits inspired and motivated. We want them to take notice of some of that organization's hallmarks of excellence, then think how they might incorporate these operationally excellent strategies into their own companies.

Tom: It's hard not to notice the love and yes, the hysteria that surrounds the Phanatic everywhere he goes. It's pretty cool to be in the middle of all that madness. When people get excited to meet you, you want to do everything in your power not to disappoint them. On top of that, fans pay their hard earned money to come to a Phillies game. You want to give them the best experience possible.

That same enthusiasm follows the Phanatic when he's out and about making appearances in the community. It's pretty awesome to visit a church carnival or school and have everyone dressed in Phillies gear jumping up and down. That enthusiasm, the creation of the Phillies loyal loving fans, is the result of our organization noticing what their fans respond to, and making the commitment to have the Phanatic deliver the joy.

Act Love

I like to joke that I have a busy job as the best friend of the Phanatic. I'm not only his best friend but I'm his chauffeur, his chef, personal trainer and his spiritual advisor. I do his laundry, answer his fan mail and tuck him into bed at night. In reality, there is a lot that happens to keep the Phanatic at the top of his game. I keep up with the maintenance of the costume, develop skit ideas and help plan the major promotions that involve the Phanatic. I have a hand in developing Phanatic merchandise ideas and help to oversee the countless special requests the Phanatic gets each and every day. It is a job that consumes my life but never feels like a job because of the love I have to make the Phanatic the best.

Evan: In our work, we often help our clients define their Paths to Excellence. As in the case of the Phanatic, clients must first decide that they truly want to be excellent. For the best organizations, this decision is genuine and authentic. It's in their DNA.

We ask them to take the concept of organizational excellence further. We help them define what excellence looks like in every area of their organization. How do you hire? What does your place of business look like? How do you answer the phone? Every aspect of their organization can be defined in terms of excellence. Once they have committed to being excellent, they can start to incorporate acts of excellence into their work culture.

Pheel the Love!

Evan: We recently visited a world-class Philadelphia school called The String Theory Charter School. From its inception, the school's founders made the decision to be excellent. There are certain standards that a charter school must meet. They are good standards, but to the folks who

113

founded String Theory, they were not good enough. They decided to raise those standards in many ways.

To begin, they chose a beautiful building to house the school located in the heart of Center City Philadelphia. They implemented a high standard of technology – there are no books in the school, only iPads. Their culture is one of respect and teachers are not seen as "enforcers of rules". The result of raising this bar? Teachers from all over the world want to teach there and the waiting list to gain admission into the school is long.

Tom: Every school, organization, community and person can decide to strive for excellence. It takes commitment, desire and passion to be great. For me, it also takes a lot of sweat. It's an exhilarating feeling to be drenched in sweat at the end of the night, knowing you've given every ounce of yourself to put on a good show and make memories. I'm not alone. Our promotions and entertainment team takes pride in sending fans home happy, too. Just like a comedian who is killing it from the stage, we know when we've had a good night. It's fun to come together at the end of the game, have a beer or two and laugh about what went on that night. Those moments I share with my co-workers makes all the sweat worth it.

CHAPTER 11: PRINCIPLE #4

THE BALLPARK *and* BEYOND:
BRIDGE THE DIVIDE BETWEEN
YOU *&* YOUR CUSTOMERS

Evan: I know the Phanatic is a rock star at the ballpark, but until I met you, I had no idea how much the Phanatic does away from the ballpark.

Tom: Well, it goes back to our first principle – The Big Smooch! – Love them First. The Phanatic wants to show his love first, and what better way to show the love than in your fans' backyard.

Evan: Like I said, the Phanatic is a rock star!

Tom: I heard rocker Gregg Allman of the Allman Brothers Band say in an interview, *"A fan came up to me and said, 'Man, I've been coming to see you play for the past 20 years!' I replied back, 'No Hoss, I've been coming to see you for the past 20 years'."*

The Phanatic has been going out to see the fans for over almost 40 years. On top of the countless community appearances at charity events, schools, hospitals and nursing homes, the Phanatic also has travelled across the country and around the world entertaining fans and sharing the love. He has been the life of the party at weddings, bar mitzvahs and charity events. Speaking of rock stars, the Phanatic has jammed with Jimmy Buffet, Billy Joel and the band Little Feat, among others, and has made guest appearances on shows like *30 Rock* and *The Goldberg's*.

One of my most memorable appearances wasn't rocking out on stage or rubbing elbows with Hollywood celebrities. It was an incredible night at the United States Justice Department Building in Washington DC. The Phanatic was a surprise guest at a private dinner for the nine Supreme Court justices. Justice Sam Alito is a big Phillies fan and the justices were hosting a dinner in his honor after a successful first year as a rookie Supreme Court justice.

I got dressed in Sandra Day O'Connor's office, who had just retired from the bench. At times, the Phillie Phanatic costume tends to take on the aroma of a laundry basket of sweaty socks so I was hoping that her office wasn't going to need to be fumigated after I left. After changing into the costume, I was summoned just outside the dining room, where dinner had just ended. I listened as Justice Stephen Breyer stood up, clinked his glass, and gave a toast.

"Sam," he began, *"Congratulations on your first year on the bench. Now, I know that you won't always agree with everyone around this table, but we invited someone tonight that you always agree with!"*

With that, the Phanatic barged into the room, and planted a big smooch on Justice Alito's smiling face. The Nine all laughed as I posed for a photo with the man of the hour, buffed the top of Justice Clarence Thomas' head with the Phanatic's fuzzy snout and bowed down in reverence to Chief Justice Roberts, who appropriately was sitting at the head of the table. I plopped myself down at the table next to Justice Thurgood Marshall's widow, Cecilia Suyat Marshall, who was a guest that night. She was amused and probably a little disgusted at the Phanatic's table manners. After a final high-five from Justice Alito, I left, leaving them laughing and kicking myself that I didn't get a couple of my parking tickets cleared up when I had the chance.

Evan: Classic, Tom! The Supreme Court is feeling the love! The Phanatic's aggressive appearance schedule is a great example of how a company/leader can show love by reaching out and going to the people. This principle is a fundamental philosophy for companies in their effort to form a personal bond with their customers. The more barriers that are torn down between your customers and your business, the more you can develop loyal loving fans for life.

Tom: And that's what the Phanatic does, whether he's stepping over seats at Citizens Bank Park or entertaining nine Supreme Court justices in Washington DC. He is the bridge to the players on the field. When a fan reaches out and touches the Phanatic, it's like they are reaching out and touching their favorite Phillie. The fans don't have the ability to rush the field to shake hands with their favorite player, but the Phanatic can initiate that personal touch by going into a row of seats and wreaking havoc. For our fans, it creates an intimate moment, a sense of belonging and a connection that can last a lifetime.

Evan: How can we go beyond the traditional bounds to touch people? Doug Conant, a former CEO of Campbell's Soup, wrote the book, *Touch Points*. In it, he talks about how leadership has its greatest impact "in the smallest moments." Doug was famous for his Doug "notes". Every day, he wrote personal thank you notes to folks in the organization. He also was a proponent of the "leading by walking around" strategy that we love so much. He would lace up his sneakers and regularly take a walk around the building for the sole purpose of bumping into people and intentionally creating touch points.

How far can we move outside the traditional bounds of our roles and touch people with love? What we learned from the Phanatic is that we can go much further. One CFO we worked with loved buying fresh fruit, bringing it into the corporate office and handing it out to his employees. Certainly, "fruit delivery" was not on his job description but he stepped out beyond his traditional role to bridge the divide that sometimes develops between leaders and the "rank and file." Not only did this act of generosity make his employees happy, it made him feel good, too. People in the company started to see him in a different light, which in turn made him more effective at his "real" job. Love does this. It makes everyone feel better and more effective.

Red Bull is amazing at this. They create and support incredible events to touch their customers and potential customers. From their World Break Dancing championships, to airplane flying competitions and their wild Flugtag, where competitors make outrageous human powered flight machines that are launched into the water from ramps thirty feet in the air, Red Bull purposefully goes all out to touch their customers in ways and places that matter to them. Take a look at your own leadership style, your marketing campaigns, and all of your potential "touch points" and see how you can radically expand them.

Imagine your organization as a ballpark; how well do you touch people personally inside your stadium? How far outside of your ballpark do you go to share your message? The Phanatic gives us permission to get up close and personal. He motivates us to go way beyond the traditional bounds of your corporate space. He brings the message right to where folks are, in places they would never expect to see him. Heck, he literally brings his company right onto your lap.

Tom: Like you said, Evan, this principle is a core fundamental for people, companies and organizations that are trying to connect with their customers and fans. Many groups have turned to social media to make this connection. Businesses have made social media platforms like Facebook and Instagram important outlets to communicate with their customers. Sports stars are bypassing the traditional news media and talk to their fans directly via their Twitter accounts. Pop stars go online to announce their newest CD release. Taylor Swift took it a step further by accepting a prom invitation from an adoring fan who reached out to her on YouTube.

I'll give Taylor credit. At least she stepped away from her computer and actually went to the prom with the guy. That's showing the love! The special magic of the Phanatic is that he creates that bond without the use of a laptop. He's not a 140-character Tweet or a six second video that gets blasted to millions of fans. He's right there in your face, delivering a personal message – I love you!

There is no substitute for delivering the personal touch. My Dad was the greatest man I've ever known. He carried himself with a quiet dignity and yet he knew how to have fun. He loved magic and used to entertain my family at birthdays and holiday parties. He eventually bought a clown costume and became a magician for hire. He became Woofus the Clown (named after the invisible "Woofus dust" he would sprinkle to make the magic happen) and performed at a handful of children's birthday parties. Dad also ran a greeting card company. Every Christmas, Dad would dress up as Santa Claus and walk through the factory handing out candy and other trinkets. Just like the Phanatic, Dad was showing the love, making a personal connection with his employees. On those days that Dad made the rounds in his Santa suit, a factory filled with machinery and skids of cartons filled with greeting cards became a little bit more intimate and a friendlier place to work.

DNA of Love

Decide Love

At some point the Phillies organization had to make a decision – should the Phillies be one of the first teams in baseball to create their own mascot character? At the time, the San Diego Padres had a guy from a local radio station running around their ballpark in a chicken costume entertaining fans with crazy antics between innings. When promotions guru at the time, Bill Giles, saw the Chicken in San Diego, an idea started to form. Bill didn't have a crystal ball or tea leaves, so he had no idea the impact a mascot would have on the Phillies organization. In fact, at the time the costume was designed, Bill had the opportunity to pay $5,200 for the costume and the copyright. Instead, he "saved" the ball club $1,300 by purchasing the costume without the copyright for $3,900. Five years later, after the Phanatic's rise in popularity, Bill and the Phillies bought the copyright from Harrison/Erickson for $250,000.

So no, Bill never envisioned what the Phanatic would later become. Instead, looking back on his decision to create the Phanatic character, Bill said, *"I just thought it would be a fun thing for our fans."*

Sometimes the best decisions are that simple.

As we have learned, the first step in creating more love is to decide. It's that simple. Go ahead, make the decision to expand the range of your touch. How far outside the "ballpark" can we go?

Notice Love

When the Phillie Phanatic made his debut, there was no plan to have him make personal appearances. It happened by accident. However, the Phillies organization quickly noticed that the green character frolicking around the Vet was becoming a big hit with the fans. They noticed that fans would stay in their seats to watch the Phanatic's dance routine in the 5th inning and they noticed the laughter coming from the stands whenever the Phanatic was out and about. They also noticed when the phones started to ring with people inquiring about how to get the Phanatic out to their Little League team's opening day celebration, or to a bank, car dealership or mall. The organization noticed some of the early appearances the Phanatic made and marveled at the size of the crowds and the excitement the Phanatic was creating.

Evan: Where are the opportunities to get beyond your "ballpark"? How do you create a culture that actively seeks these opportunities? As a leader, how do you purposefully go out into your world? Once, we were coaching a senior leader, helping him get out into his world. Like most of us, he routinely got caught up with the work that cluttered his schedule each day – emails, meetings, phone calls, etc. He was losing touch with his employees because of the demands on his schedule. He did very well with structure, so we came up with "Thank You Thursdays". Each Thursday became his time to go out and thank people who rarely get thanked in his organization. Simple!

Act Love

The Phillies did the right thing. They acted and thank goodness they did, or I would not be writing this book. They made the Phanatic available for outside appearances and quickly hired a back-up for Dave Raymond. Eleven years later, with the outside appearance schedule in full swing, they hired me to become Dave Raymond's full-time back-up. The club invested in a Phillie Phanatic van so that I can now pull up to an appearance as Clark Kent, get dressed in the back and pop out like Superman. We have a full-time person who handles the bookings and who sorts through the many appearance requests. Today, I have three talented guys assisting with Phanatic outside appearances. We perform at every kind of event imaginable. I used to say that the Phanatic does any kind of appearance except for a funeral but I was wrong. A couple of years ago, the Phanatic was invited to a funeral. I had my doubts that going to a funeral as the Phanatic was crossing the line of good taste, but in the end, the family and friends of the deceased (a huge Phillies fan...obviously), laughed and smiled and made the whole thing seem right. That appearance typifies our principle – the ballpark and BEYOND!

Evan: Nothing builds bridges within organizations better than great communication. Frequent communication connects people, whereas poor communication creates a divide. We do a great deal of work with organizations who have gone through mergers and we have witnessed the behaviors and attitudes that contribute to successful integrations. One way to bridge the divide is communication. We hear the same message repeatedly: People feel loved when they are informed. So over communicate. Tell them that it's complicated. Tell them that you don't have all of the answers yet. Just tell them. People would rather hear the truth, even if it's not what they want to hear. It's the best way to bridge the divide.

Pheel the Love!

Tom: The Phanatic has two places he shares the love – at the ballpark and beyond the ballpark. If you are keeping track at home, that means just about everywhere! It's a pretty cool feeling to know that when I'm reaching out to a fan in the stands or high-fiving a kid at an outside appearance, I'm representing the connection that person is making with our entire organization. As we stated with our first principle, it is about loving them first but it is also about bridging the gap between the organization and our fans. We get huge rewards by going out beyond our "ballparks".

CHAPTER 12: PRINCIPLE #5
AVOID *the* WHAMMY!:
PUT THE RIGHT PEOPLE IN
the RIGHT POSITIONS

Evan: So, Tom, what's the whammy?

Tom: The whammy is a move the Phillie Phanatic does to put a hex on the other team. Most of the time, he's stands on the dugout and tries to put the whammy on the other team's pitcher before he throws a pitch. The Phanatic spits in his hands, rubs them together, bends slightly at the knees and then shakes his hands in a menacing fashion towards the opposing player.

Evan: Does it work?

Tom: Absolutely... well, most of the time. Jose Reyes was a shortstop for the New York Mets who batted first in the lineup. He would warm up in the on-deck circle just before the game started. We had a routine we did every time the Mets were in town. The Phanatic would walk over to Reyes and get ready to put the whammy on him. Just as the Phanatic was ready to cast his spell, the clever shortstop would step out of the way, trying to dodge the imaginary voodoo hex heading his way. If Reyes led off the game with an out, I knew that the whammy had worked. If he reached base than I knew that he had avoided the whammy. Get it?

Evan: I got it, Tom, but what does the whammy have to do with *Pheeling the Love*?

Tom: *Pheeling the Love* is all about helping other people succeed, but it's sometimes easier said than done. There can be traps along the way – the whammy – that cripples our effort to succeed.

One of the best ways to help people succeed is to put them in a position to succeed. As parents, we help our kids find that thing in life that they love to do. We sign them up for baseball, soccer, dance and piano lessons; any sport and after-school activity we can think of, hoping that they find one that they love. As they grow older, we nudge them towards those careers that we know they will excel in, and encourage them to follow their dreams.

As leaders, when we genuinely care for people and learn what makes them tick, what makes them happy, we can show them the love by putting them in a position to succeed.

Evan: I guess whoever hired you to be the Phillie Phanatic "avoided the whammy?"

Tom: You got that right! As I related earlier, I was the class clown growing up, a Phillie Phanatic wannabe. I loved Bugs Bunny and Daffy Duck, watched *The Three Stooges* every day after school and collected Mad magazines. I lived and breathed Philadelphia sports and plastered the walls in my bedroom with posters of Dr. J and Mike Schmidt. I was our high school mascot, the Hawk, and had a job selling (and dressing up in) Halloween costumes before graduating from college. After graduation, I stumbled across an anonymous want ad the Phillies had placed in the Sunday paper. It read simply, "Mascots Wanted." I interviewed, auditioned and landed my dream job. That day, I went to the bank and ran into my friend's mom, Mrs. Dougherty, who worked there.

"Hi, Mrs. Dougherty."

"Hi there, Tommy. What's new?"

"Well, I just got a new job."

"Let me guess. You're going to be the Phillie Phanatic."

As hard as it is to believe, that's a true story. I think Mrs. Dougherty should leave the banking business and find a job as a tarot card reader. The point is, I found that thing in life I was meant to do, the Phillies noticed and put me in a position to succeed.

But I'm just one example of how the Phillies avoid the whammy and put people in the right positions to succeed. As I mentioned earlier, there are three guys who also make appearances as the Phanatic. I talked about Matt Mehler earlier. Matt has been performing as the Phanatic for over 20 years. Before becoming the back-up Phanatic, Matt acted in plays and dinner theater productions. Soon after Matt joined the Phillies, he became the master of disguises and the perfect foil for the Phanatic. Throughout the baseball season, Matt dresses up as an umpire and sneaks out onto the field between innings. After being taunted by the Phanatic, Matt will rip off his shirt and pants revealing a costume underneath. Under his ump's uniform Matt has dressed as a

Spanish bull fighter, Ike Turner, Pitbull, Ricky Martin and a crowd favorite – the Irish umpire, revealing an Irish kilt, green suspenders and neon green hair. Together, the Phanatic and the Irish umpire fumble through an Irish jig before the real umpire comes over and kicks Matt off the field.

Matt has found his groove and we have a blast together coming up with skit ideas and other crazy characters for him to play. The Phanatic's act is better because Matt is in his lane, naturally tapping his acting abilities and having fun doing it.

My other assistant, Mike Alexander, has also been performing as the Phanatic for over 20 years. Mike teaches high school level special needs kids and is another guy who found his passion. Mike has a huge heart and is maybe more qualified than anyone else to spread the love as the Phanatic. He's instinctively compassionate. It's in his DNA. When he steps into the Phanatic's sneakers, dishing out hugs and high-fives comes naturally.

Troy Sattin is the young buck of our group. Troy has been "phanaticing" for six years and loves what he does. He's built like a brick house and takes his conditioning seriously. In addition to his duties as the Phanatic, Troy heads up the Phillies Phitness program, educating kids about the importance of exercise and eating healthy.

Our Phanatic team is a perfect example of the Phillies creating an atmosphere to help people find that thing they love to do. I'm happy to say that those types of success stories run rampant throughout the Phillies organization. Employees love coming to work because they are doing what they were tailored-made to do. It's a gift that an organization can give its employees, and a great way to show them the love.

Putting people in the right position means that their jobs need to be an expression of who they are. By tapping into an individual's talent and passion, organizations succeed. In *Good to Great,* author Jim Collins, makes this point so well. He writes about the importance of having the right people in the right positions. Here's the really cool part of this idea. When we do have the right people in the right positions, they are intrinsically motivated. They don't need a lot of "managing." This is a common theme to our love proposition. When loved, people will want to do their best, they will put forth extra effort, they will be proud of their work and the organizations they work for.

One of the main ways to create love is to give people an opportunity to do what they do best. In turn, the love comes back to the organization because they are doing what they do best, with passion and love. The payoffs are priceless.

DNA of Love

Decide Love

Creating an environment that enables employees to be the best they can be starts at the top of the organization. In my years with the Phillies, that type of positive leadership has come from Bill Giles and David Montgomery, who have been involved with running the club since 1981. Hiring qualified, passionate people and putting them in a position to succeed has been the cornerstone of their leadership philosophy. We have a new president, Andy MacPhail, who shares their philosophy. All three understand that when people are happy doing what they are doing and have a voice in decisions that are made, it makes for a productive and positive work environment. That type of leadership is genuine and can't be manufactured.

I have already mentioned lunchtime as a good example of how the Phillies maintain a family-type working environment. Everyone sits together; there is no hierarchy. We share stories about life, our kids and what's hot on TV. We might even talk about baseball. I remember one day I was sitting at a table that included David Montgomery. The Phillies were in Florida at Spring Training and we were discussing a story that ran in the paper that morning. John Kruk had hit a foul ball that smashed the window of a car parked in the parking lot at Jack Russell Stadium. The car belonged to an elderly woman, who never missed a home spring training game. Ruth Smith was sitting at our table. Ruth has been one of our phone center operators for over 25 years. She offered that wouldn't it be great if John Kruk signed the ball for that woman. David agreed, made a call to Clearwater, and made arrangements for Kruk to sign the ball. The next day, a follow up story ran in the newspaper about the woman and her meeting with Kruk. Ruth was thrilled that her idea during a casual conversation at lunch had resulted in such a feel-good story.

Deciding to be an organization that brings out the best in people is the first step in avoiding the whammy.

Notice Love

The only way to put the right people in the right positions is to notice them, listen to them, talk with them, and really get to know them. It won't take long to find out what makes them tick and what makes them happy and where their talent lies. When I was hired as the full-time back-up to Dave Raymond, I spent time in the phone center with Ruth and other phone operators, answering calls and selling individual game tickets. I loved it! I was talking Phillies baseball with other Phillies fans over the phone and selling them tickets. How cool was that? I was on a roll, so I asked my supervisor that instead of answering calls as they came in, would they let me make sales phone calls to Philadelphia companies and help sell our group seating areas. Soon, our director of marketing noticed that I was pretty fired up representing the Phillies, not only as the Phanatic at appearances but on the phone selling tickets and drumming up business. He plucked me from the phone center and gave me a job in our promotions department. I worked with radio stations, giving out tickets and staging radio-sponsored promotions. On top of my duties as the Phanatic, I worked in our video control room spinning tunes between innings and working with Dave Raymond on skit ideas. I really started to feel like I was utilizing my talents and contributing to the club in a positive way.

Being noticed and having someone discover my talents, maybe even before I realized I had those talents, not only made me a better employee. It made me a happier person.

Evan: One of the strongest mentors in my life is my friend Bob Megill. Bob and I have had hundreds of conversations. Most of them are focused around him helping me become a better person. On one call, Bob was helping me appreciate my own talents. He asked me if I knew what my gifts were. I wasn't sure what he meant, so he explained that our gifts are those things which come easy and naturally to us – almost second nature.

We believe that allowing people to work "in their gifts" is a way to be loving. To do this, we must first notice their "giftedness." Then we must trust and give them opportunities to exercise their gifts. An organization brimming with people working full-out in their giftedness is love in full gear.

Act Love

Putting the right people in the right positions to succeed is a win-win for everybody. The company profits when employees are energized and doing what they do best, and employees are happier in their jobs. But life isn't always that easy. We can get "whammied" and fall back into bad habits. We get caught up with what we have to do first and put other people's needs and wants on the back burner. E-mails, voicemails, meetings, kid's schedules and everything else gets in the way of truly being there for others. It sounds easy enough – put the right people in the right positions to succeed - but unless we are truly caring and in-tune to what makes the people around us tick, then nothing will change. To be caring is to love. The first thing we need to do before we can put people in positions to succeed is to care. We need to listen and be present when they need us. It's only then when we can act.

Pheel the Love!

Tom: When you are employed by someone else, it means that you are always being evaluated. You are measured in many ways. Are you on time? Are you getting the job done? Do you work well with others? When our marketing director promoted me to a coveted spot in our promotions department, I felt great. When you are put in a position to succeed, it means that someone believes in you. That is a great feeling.

133

After the 1993 season, the original Phanatic, Dave Raymond went on to start his own business. There was no guarantee that I would take over as the lead performer, even though I had been Dave's back-up for five years. When the Phillies quickly inserted me into the job, I knew I had the support of the organization. What a feeling that is! It's empowering to have people believe in you. It also motivated me to not let them down. I took more ownership of what I needed to do and how I wanted the Phanatic character to evolve. I became more confident and satisfied, not only at work but in life. All those good feelings, all of that love, came about because someone saw something in me and put me in a position to succeed.

As it turns out, Mrs. Dougherty knew all along.

CHAPTER 13: PRINCIPLE #6
GIVE'M *the* BELLY WHOMP:
MAKE *it* FUN!

Evan: I know what you are thinking. *"Here we go again. Another book that says that you have to have fun in the workplace. If you have fun, you'll be productive. Yada, yada, yada…"*

I get it. I'm sure most of you have held a job where the boss reads a book about improving performance in the office, and the next thing you know you are rewarded with a visit from the local ice cream truck and a new casual Friday policy.

Tom: Hey, don't knock casual Fridays. The Phanatic is a big fan. He never wears pants so every day is casual Fridays.

Evan: Good one, Tom. Listen, I'm a firm believer in fun and have written and studied about the importance of play. I'm hoping that we can offer some fresh ideas about what it means to truly lead a playful life.

Tom: It's pretty easy for me to have fun at work. I'm a mascot for crying out loud! The Phanatic's idea of fun is hitting someone in the face with a whipped cream pie or pants-ing Matt when he's dressed as the opposing team's third base coach. The Phanatic is at his best when he's letting things fly and having fun.

But it seems a little selfish for the Phanatic to have all the fun. That's why it's fun for me to involve my co-workers in Phanatic skits between innings. When employees get in on the act, we all have fun.

Evan: You make a great point Tom. In my first book, *It's O.K. to Play!*, we talk a lot about the concept of playmates. We ask, at what point did we stop thinking of the people in our lives as playmates? We wonder what would change if we saw our bosses, our co-workers and our customers as playmates, just like we saw our friends as kids? One of the main ways to make work more fun is to invite others to play. People love being asked to doing something cool, new or important. Just the act of asking other people to play often creates more support for your idea or initiative.

Tom: The Phillies have a promotion called Retro Night, where we roll back the clock and celebrate a certain time period in the team's history. Our employees get in on the act. They dress in costumes from that time period. When we celebrated the sixties, we had a James Bond look-a-like, the cast of Gilligan's Island, hippies and the band, the Monkeys, among others, all dancing along with the Phanatic. One year, we created a dance team called the Red Soul Line Dancers with six guys from our front office. All season, they would come out between innings and bust a move wearing red zoot suits and matching red derby hats. You'd never have seen these guys on a Bruno Mars music video, but they weren't too bad.

One year, the Toronto Blue Jays were forced to play three home games against the Phillies in Philadelphia. There was an international conference being held in Toronto and so the Blue Jays were the home team at Citizens Bank Park. The Phanatic wanted to make them feel at home, so we dressed six of my co-workers in Canadian Mountie uniforms and marched them out onto the field between innings. The Phanatic hopped off his ATV and tried desperately to get them to dance. The fake Mounties stayed in character, with frowns on their faces and standing at attention. When the Village People's song, "YMCA" came on, the Mounties broke character and started spelling out the letters, YMCA and danced all around. We decided not do an encore performance the second night when we found out that Canadians are not too fond of the Mounties being made to look silly. The last thing the Phanatic wanted to do was spark an international incident.

Evan: Do you come up with your own skit ideas?

Tom: I do, and this is where the *Pheel the Love!* comes in, Evan. As we mentioned in the last principle, the Phillies put me in the right position to succeed. Once they did that, I could go out and have fun! They put their trust in me that I will provide family-style entertainment and be an ambassador of love for the organization.

That trust is there even when I'm out of costume. The Phillies have allowed me to expand the brand in ways that I think will benefit the Phanatic and the entire organization. When you are given that kind of freedom, it can spark creativity. When the creative juices are flowing, and you are working on projects that you are emotionally invested in, it creates an atmosphere of excitement and fun throughout the organization.

I've worked with people throughout the organization to extend the Phanatic's brand. With the help of our Fan Development department, we created a children's reading program that touches over 100,000 kids a year. The program encourages kids to read for at least 20 minutes each day and emphasizes that reading is fun. Our Video Services department has worked with me to produce four different Phanatic home videos. Our video team had a blast putting these films together. They challenged each other to come up with cool special effects and fun ideas to add to the production. In 2010, the Phillies launched a public arts program that involved custom-painted Phanatic statues scattered throughout the city. We auctioned off the statues and raised over $250,000 for Phillies Charities. Not only did our local artists have fun creating Phillie Phanatic statues painted like the Liberty Bell, Ben Franklin and an astronaut (among others), but our Community Relations department was jazzed watching the bids for the statues go through the roof during the on-line auction.

All of these projects and the skits that I get to perform during the game come from a place of fun. If it's fun, and you are given the freedom to try it, go for it!

Evan: Tom, you and the Phillies are hitting on so many keys to the concept of play. For my team, like love, play is all about unleashing the fullest potential of people. We have learned that in play we do our best. If we are serious about something, then the best thing we can do is play with it. People think play is being frivolous, but it's not. Think of a surgeon playing. For him or her, play doesn't mean throwing a scalpel around the room or skipping around the operating table. It means being fully engaged, paying attention, exploring, looking for the best result and being wide open to innovation. That is play at its best.

When the Phillies give you freedom, they are allowing you room to play and letting your best talents shine through. The play piece adds the joy to what you are doing. Joy is a very powerful force. It allows us to do our best work and feel good about ourselves. Look at all the love and loyalty you have for the Phillies because they have given you this freedom and support.

Tom: It really is a blast to bring people into the Phanatic's world and have fun. However, just like our unfortunate hot dog bomb scare, sometimes things don't go as planned. One year, Lady Gaga appeared at the Grammys in an egg. She was carried down the red carpet by guys dressed like gladiators and broke out of the egg on stage for her performance. When I watched Lady Gaga that night, I knew right away that the Phanatic could have fun with it. We had an egg custom made for the Phanatic

– obviously much bigger than Gaga's - to accommodate the Phanatic's wide girth. I didn't want to be the one having all the fun, so I enlisted the help of six employees to dress in tunics and be the ones to carry the egg onto the field. So on Opening Day, between innings, the guys hoisted the egg over their shoulders, onto the field and placed it in front of the visitor's dugout. When Gaga's song, "Born This Way" blared out over the PA system, out popped Galapagos Islands' pop sensation, Lady "Pha Pha." We duplicated Lady Gaga's Grammy outfit, right down to the yellow two-piece dress, floppy hat and blond pony-tailed wig. The crowd loved it when I gyrated in front of the St. Louis Cardinals bench and swirled my pony-tail around and around in front of the player in the on-deck circle. Before exiting the field, I noticed that something was wrong. The music had stopped and pitcher Roy Halladay was standing behind the mound, hands on his hips and looking none too happy. My six fellow employees – the ones I decided to bring into the Phanatic's world of fun – had forgotten to take the egg off the field, causing a delay in the action. They eventually scrambled over to the dugout and made a hasty exit off the field with the egg. I was left standing there, in my yellow dress and floppy hat, being stared down by Roy Halladay. Sorry about that, Roy, I was just having fun.

PHEEL *the* LOVE!

DNA of Love

Decide Love

An atmosphere of fun has to come from the top and be part of an organization's mission. Like all of our principles of love, it has to be genuine. It's a philosophy that can't be faked. The fun we are talking about comes from loving what we do. This is the real fun. It's not just about doing fun things at work, like a fun Band-Aid. This is a much deeper fun and joy. We can't have this level of fun and joy if we don't love what we are doing. We can't fake it. It means we have to take responsibility to find work that we love. We can't have the benefits of love–the fun, the joy and the success–if we don't love what we are doing. If you are not feeling the love at your work, then it's your own personal journey to find and create that love. You may have to leave to find the love, but most likely there is another path; creating the love right where you are.

Tom: When Bill Giles arrived in Philadelphia, he noticed that people weren't having much fun at the ballpark. The Phillies suffered an epic collapse in 1964, blowing a seven and a half game lead with twelve games to play, and lost the pennant. The mood of the club was gloomy as the '60s gave way to the '70s. When Veterans Stadium opened in 1971, Bill took the opportunity to put fun back in the ballpark. He incorporated crazy first ball deliveries on Opening Day and began a series of wacky promotions and crazy stunts throughout the season at the Vet. The stadium had dancing water fountains behind the outfield fence and huge electronic scoreboards flashed fun animations after big plays. The "Hot Pants Patrol" ushered fans to their seats and there was a motorized cart in the shape of a baseball that brought pitchers in from the bullpen. There was a new atmosphere at Phillies games and it was fun. The key was Bill Giles. He had the Love DNA in him.

That philosophy was still in play when Bill decided to bring a mascot to Philadelphia. The Phanatic was just one part of the game day experience that made going to a Phillies game fun. Bill later took control of baseball operations and put together a team in 1993 that went to the World Series. I co-authored a book about that season and interviewed each player ten years later. To a man, they all said that they never had so much fun playing the game as they did that season. That fun translated into wins as most of the players on the team had career years in '93. Bill Giles said that he got a rare phone call from New York Yankees owner George Steinbrenner that year. George told Bill that he envied the club Bill put together because of the personalities of the players on that team and the fun atmosphere that permeated the clubhouse.

Bill Giles learned at an early age that having fun is a key ingredient of success. Dave Raymond was nervous on the day the Phanatic made his debut at Veterans Stadium. He knew all about the hard-nosed reputation that the Philadelphia's sports fans had earned and wondered what kind of reaction the new mascot would receive. He ran into Bill just before the game and asked him what exactly he should do on that first night.

Bill said, *"David, just go out and have fun."* Not only was Bill advising Dave that night to have fun, but it was as if he was directing the entire organization to do the same.

As leaders, we set the tone for the organization. Your attitude and demeanor have more of an impact than your words. How do we be playful? How do we give more freedom? How do we give people a chance to take inspired action? Without Bill Giles' vision and willingness to let go, there would be no Phanatic. The DNA of Love was planted in the Phanatic by Bill.

Notice Love

Today, people live their work more than ever. When companies downsize, workers are expected to pick up the slack and take on more responsibilities. They are attached to their smart phones and stay connected to the office even when they are at home. Vacations aren't really vacations when your manager can reach you by email even when you are lying on the beach. At some point, people have to have fun. All work and no play is no way to go through life.

It is pretty simple to notice a workplace devoid of fun. As leaders, are we being too serious and too controlling? Where can we let go? Where can we be more upbeat? Where can we give others freedom to create? How can you empower people? Look at your policies and procedures. Are they imbued with love or are they coming from a place of control? Where can you bring a little Bill Giles into the picture? Is there a Phanatic out there that you can emulate?

Bill saw the concept of the mascot working elsewhere and had the foresight to bring it to the Phillies. What do you see working in another venue or corporation? What can you try? How can you bring more excellence to your organization? There are tons of opportunities to bring more life, more joy, more play, more excellence and more fun to your world. Go ahead, take a chance and give it a ride!

Act Love

The amount to which a person is respected, trusted and put in a position to succeed will determine how much fun they have on the job. Establishing a workplace that allows the free flow of ideas and creativity will lead to the experience of fun. There is nothing wrong with putting a ping-pong table in the break room or organizing a company picnic. That's all good. If it feels right – go for it! But creating a fun atmosphere at work needs to be more than that.

All too often what is created in organizations is not love, but fear. When people are micro-managed, they become afraid to share new ideas and try new things. The fear takes away the empowerment. If people are afraid to make mistakes, they will not take risks and instead, they will play it safe. More importantly, their creativity and passion will be stifled. The love can't exist if the leadership creates a fear-filled culture.

We have to create an atmosphere where people feel free to be creative, to do their best and have fun. If you are walking around, looking and acting serious all the time, how much fun are you going to allow in your organization? Put a smile on your face, even if you aren't always feeling that way. Lighten up and have fun with people. Encourage them to enjoy themselves.

A key element of creating a fun culture is our ability to laugh at ourselves as leaders. Having a lightness about ourselves and being able to laugh at our own mistakes will certainly free up people in your organization to do the same. It is a great gift you can give others and yourself.

Pheel the Love!

For the Phanatic, if it's not fun, it's not worth doing. The Phanatic was born to create fun. He makes baseball games more fun with his antics and he livens up the party when he makes outside appearances. However, the Phanatic wouldn't be the life of the party if he wasn't given the permission to go out and have fun. When an atmosphere of fun and play is encouraged, everyone benefits. It makes me happy to share that fun. The more people I bring into the Phanatic's fun, the better I feel. Having fun is good for business and good for the soul.

Play is all about experimentation, being curious and taking positive risks. When we add more play to our processes, we are increasing the possibility of being more successful and achieving our goals. So remember to Give'm the Belly Whomp and make it fun!

CHAPTER 14: PRINCIPLE #7
7TH *inning* CELEBRATION:
DANCE *and* BE OPTIMISTIC
NO MATTER WHAT THE SCORE

The famous leadership guru Peter Drucker coined the phrase, *"Culture eats strategy for lunch."* He is alluding to the powerful impact culture has on determining the course of any organization. How many organizations do you know that are truly optimistic? Do they respond optimistically in the face of a crisis? Are their leaders encouraging, supportive and upbeat? Is the work environment a happy place to be? If our whole purpose is to create the kinds of places we love, then we believe that being optimistic, no matter what the score, is critical.

Evan: When you're in costume, is it hard to always be "up", always be optimistic?

Tom: No, every time I put that head on, the Phanatic takes over. It's magic. I might be having a rough day and maybe not feeling up to being the life of the party but when I put that costume on, it's Showtime!

Evan: We talked about people's Outward Expression of Optimism in Principle One. What amazes me about the Phanatic is that it seems like every movement he makes conveys optimism, happiness and joy.

Tom: Well, as we said earlier, the Phanatic's Outward Expression of Optimism is to hug, high-five, smooch and DANCE! The Phanatic has danced from Day 1. He dances on the field, dances on the dugout and he will bust a move if you run into the Phanatic at an appearance. The highlight of the night for me comes at the end of the 7th inning. The music comes on and the Phanatic dances on top of the Phillies dugout. Sometimes we have kids or dance groups scheduled to join the Phanatic, but most times I get to randomly pull a fan up from the crowd. Most nights, I feel like Bruce Springsteen in the *Born in the USA* video when he selects Courtney Cox out of the crowd to join him on stage and dance.

Evan: This might be our most important principle, Tom. No matter what life throws at you, the good and the bad, and no matter what the score – dance and be optimistic! I have learned a lot working with you on this book. I have had down moments and I ask myself, *"What would the Phanatic do?"* I imagine the little green guy in my brain. My nature is to be pessimistic, but the Phanatic is optimistic. Having the Phanatic with me gives me a way to choose to be optimistic. I know I'm not alone. There are a lot of us worriers out there in life. It's great to know I can keep some part of myself and that no matter what the score, he can come out and be optimistic. Thanks, Phanatic.

Tom: And that's the Phanatic's job! There are times, when I go out for the 7th inning dance, the Phillies are losing badly. But when the Phanatic appears and makes his way to the dugout, I can hear the laughter, the *"Yo, Phanatic!"* calls and can feel the energy level rise. It's as if the fans forget how bad things are going that night and relax and enjoy the Phanatic. Of course, singing "Take Me Out to the Ballgame" during the 7th inning stretch has been around a lot longer than the Phanatic. Our fans sing that traditional song a half inning before the Phanatic does his dance. In a way, the rituals are similar. Even if the hometown team is losing, fans stand up and sing as one.

Evan: It's also important to celebrate success. As part of my consulting practice, we offer a great leadership program called Celebration™. The purpose of the program is to recognize that too often, we don't stop to celebrate our successes in our work. We just keep moving on. Sometimes there are spontaneous celebrations, but our program recommends purposely stopping to celebrate, and encourages organizations to create celebration rituals. The Phanatic comes out every 7th inning regardless of the score. The same principle applies if organizations want to capture the full power of the Phanatic. The concept of celebration goes beyond champagne and balloons. Celebrating is a way to mark things: to mark time and to mark accomplishments. Every Monday my office has a WAM meeting, which stands for Weekly Accountability Meetings. It's a chance to review all of our activity from the week before and assess how we did. Where did we excel? What do we need to change? Understand that the WAM meetings are encouraging in nature, and are meant to help keep us on track and continue to improve. WAM is a celebration. Celebrations are powerful, loving tools in any organization.

Tom: In baseball, we know how to celebrate success. When the Phillies won the World Series in 2008, boy did we celebrate. After Brad Lidge struck out Tampa Ray's Eric Hinske for the final out, the Phanatic rushed out of the dugout and collapsed to the ground as the fireworks exploded over the ballpark. I was handed the championship flag and waved it back and forth before handing it off to first baseman Ryan Howard, who paraded it around the field with his teammates.

The celebration spilled into the locker room where the champagne corks flew and beer was sprayed. The Phillies organization had a post-game tent party in the parking lot that rocked into the wee hours of the morning. Two days later, millions of fans joined the celebration and crowded the streets to witness the parade down Broad Street. I was on the first truck, perched on top of a wooden platform with the best view of all. What a sight to behold! Fans were everywhere and love was all around. I couldn't help thinking back to my first Phillies victory parade which I viewed hanging from a statue. Championship parades are one ritual that I wouldn't mind celebrating every year!

PHEEL *the* LOVE!

DNA of Love

Decide Love

Every organization has to decide what kind of company it wants to be. Organizations face challenges all the time. There is no way around it. The leaders of an organization choose what kind of culture they will have. Some people are naturally optimistic, but many are not. What kind of culture are you creating? Are you being optimistic no matter what the score? The Phanatic teaches us that we can make the decision to be optimistic, especially in the face of hardship. This decision has great power to influence everyone we touch, and ourselves.

Senior leaders play an important role in leading an organization. In our experience, the most important role they play is modeling the values and culture that the organization aspires to. We can't expect an organization to be anything other than what their senior leaders demonstrate on a daily level. When facing a critical challenge to their organization, the senior leadership team should see it as a chance to be optimistic if they want their organization to be optimistic. This takes great courage and fortitude especially if that challenge causes hardship to the organization.

In his book *Onward: How Starbucks Fought for its Life without Losing its Soul*, CEO and founder Howard Schultz talks about firing his largest stockholder because he wanted to cut employee benefits during the recession downturn. For Shultz, the benefits were key to their values and culture of

151

caring for their employees. In that moment of concern, he stood for his values in the face of great potential loss. He viewed the loss of corporate values as a greater threat than the potential loss of revenue.

It goes beyond your "ballpark" as we have learned. The decision you make about the tone of your organization will seep out into the world. What do people feel when they see your logo on a letterhead, on a billboard or in the newspaper? What emotions are tapped?

When people see the Phillies logo, many words and feelings come to mind – fun, baseball, tradition, family entertainment, memories, great wins, some losses, spectacular ballpark, and so on. When they see the Phanatic, hopefully they think happy thoughts and smile (and maybe forget about some of the losses…). The Phanatic helps to reinforce all the good things associated with Phillies baseball.

The Phillies have been around since 1883. That's a long time. We were the first team in professional sports to reach 10,000 losses. That's a lot of losses. But I do believe that when fans see the "P" logo that represents Phillies baseball, they don't think of those 10,000 losses. They think of fun at the ballpark and family memories. They might think of the positive impact the team has had in the community. Outreach programs like the *Phanatic About Reading* program and the RBI program, our inner-city youth baseball organization, strengthen that bond between the team and our fans. The Phillies organization has raised

152

millions of dollars for local and national charities over the years, directly affecting people who need help the most. Smaller moments like catching a foul ball at a game or running into the Phanatic on the concourse can cement that bond and make fans for life.

Notice Love

It's not too difficult to notice when your "crowd" needs a lift. For the Phanatic, when the team is losing, the mood in the stands drags and fans sit on their hands. You can also see it in your own environment. You can see when folks are having a tough day at work. There might be days you can't seem to get anything done. Maybe things are difficult on the home front or days you just don't feel appreciated. Everyone has days like this. It's everyone's responsibility to notice when our friends, neighbors and co-workers are having "one of those days." It is an act of love to dance, be optimistic and to bring that person "up."

Act Love

The Phillie Phanatic dances no matter what the score. When the chips are down, the Phanatic is there to lift you up. He will dance, belly whomp, and tease the opposing team. When the crowd is down and the game needs a jolt of energy, the Phanatic will take off his jersey and streak in his birthday suit across the outfield. Watching a naked Phillie

Phanatic run around the field with the song "The Streak" playing over the loudspeakers can't help but make you smile.

Is there a way you can ritualize positivity? Is there a way to create pockets of optimism in your organization? What can you do on a regular basis to create confidence, faith and a positive attitude? How do you celebrate accomplishments? How do you regularly reward and recognize people? Are you walking around, giving folks a pat on the back, a smile, some recognition, no matter what the score?

As an organization, the Phillies make sure that their employees are noticed and appreciated. I am happy to say that I have three championship rings. Two rings represent the Phillies National League Championships in 1993 and 2009 and the other ring is a happy reminder of the 2008 World Series championship. That is the big one with enough bling to make Beyoncé jealous. Every front office employee received a ring right down to the ground crew guys in Clearwater. It's a great example of how everyone in the organization is meant to feel that we are all part of the same team and that we are all appreciated.

Pheel the Love!

When our own personal Outward Expression of Optimism can lift another person's spirit, we are truly *Pheeling the Love*. If the Phillies are losing, it's a great feeling for me to lift the energy of the crowd and allow them to forget the score for a while. It's an even better feeling when the team is winning and I get to lead the celebration.

That feel-good feeling happens in the business world as well. If we are positive and optimistic as an organization, then we lift the spirits of everyone we touch: our customers, our employees and co-workers. The love we feel at work comes home with us, too. It touches our significant others, our children, and our friends. If we can build optimistic, loving organizations, we are having a tremendous impact on the world. We are putting a smile on the world, just like the Phillie Phanatic does every day.

It feels good to be on the receiving end of that love and appreciation. To this day, my fellow employees and I wear our championship rings and tell stories about the good old days. Those rings are a symbol of love that remind us of the good times and that we are all appreciated. When we look at those championship rings, we *Pheel the Love!*

PART 4

THE
Big CLOSE

CHAPTER 15
THE *love* 15™

Blueprints. Carpenters can easily build a house if they have a set of blueprints to follow. The Love 15™ is a set of carefully crafted questions designed to help you build a company where team members and customers start to *Pheel the Love!* By asking and answering these questions, you will begin to build a blueprint for love in your organization.

The LOVE 15™

1. Do people love coming to work here? What can we do to create a workplace that people love?

2. Team members want their work to matter and have meaning. Is our business connected to a higher purpose? Does everyone understand what that higher purpose is?

3. Do our customers love our product or service? What can we do to help them love us more?

4. People love to be associated with excellence. As an organization, are we striving for excellence in everything we do? How can we be more excellent?

5. Love flourishes in an environment of respect. How do we ensure that everyone feels respected?

6. We all want to contribute and do our best. Does our culture encourage everyone to tap into their passion and fully utilize their talents?

7. Feeling valued is critical to fostering an environment of love. Do our people feel valued and well-compensated?

8. People like feeling a part of something. How can we create a more inclusive and collaborative environment?

9. People thrive when they are learning and progressing. How do we create more opportunities for people to learn and develop?

10. People are influenced by their physical environment. Is our space welcoming, inspiring and functional?

11. Everyone has unique skills, abilities and interests. Do we have the right people in the right positions?

12. People want to be noticed. What can we do to make our team members and customers feel special?

13. Getting the chance to work with other well-meaning, high-performing people is exciting. What can we do to ensure that our organization is chock-full of smart, nice people?

14. Optimism is an awesome quality in any organization. To what extent are we optimistic in our attitude and actions?

15. Laughter, humor and joy are powerful drivers of love. What can we do to make our day and our interactions more fun and enjoyable?

The Love 15™ in Action

There are many ways to put The Love 15™ into action. Here are a list of practical options:

One-On-Ones

It is common for managers to hold regular one-on-one meetings with their direct reports. The Love 15™ can be a centerpiece for those meetings. Select one of The Love 15™ questions to focus upon – for example: #4. *As an organization, are we striving for excellence in everything we do? How can we be more excellent?* Allow this question to fuel your conversation. We suggest using the *Start, Stop, Continue* model to frame your responses. So, in terms of this question, ask yourself what do we want to *Start* doing that would make us more excellent, what do we want to *Stop* doing that would make us more excellent and what do we want to *Continue* doing to maintain our excellence?

Culture Surveys

Culture surveys are designed to collect metrics in any number of areas. Why not consider using The Love 15™ as your assessment tool to see where your organization stands today? In addition to having participants select a numeric response, be sure to leave a space for open-ended comments or suggestions related to each question. This will help you to "crowd-source" your way to love using recommendations and ideas from your entire team.

Your Brand

The Love 15™ can be a very powerful tool to assist you in cultivating your brand and your ever-important reputation in the marketplace. Every company has a brand, whether they know what it is or not. We encourage clients to proactively define what they want their brand "promise" to be and then…wait for it…this is the courageous part - share it directly with their customers. Tell them, *"This is who we are striving to be for you."* Then ask them, *"How are we doing?"* In conducting these "live" client visits (we encourage you to do them in person when possible) you will not only strengthen the relationships you have with your clients, you will learn where you need to improve. Remember that your goal is for your customers to feel loved by you. Imagine how great your customers will feel when you promise to do everything in your power to love them. What customer wouldn't love you for doing that?

Leadership Inventory

During our leadership retreats we showcase a box. We say, *"Inside this box is THE most powerful leadership tool known to mankind."* Then we ask participants to guess what's inside. One CEO, took a shot at guessing the answer. He said, *"It's a mirror."* He was alluding to one of the most important qualities of leadership, self-reflection.

The Love 15™ can be a very effective tool for self-reflection. On a regular basis, take time to reflect on each question. How are you doing? What is making the most difference? The Love 15™ will provide you with a compass to guide your weekly activities.

If you decide to take on The Love 15™, we think you will not only start *Pheeling the Love!* but you'll start seeing the payoffs that love produces.

CHAPTER 16

PHEEL *the* LOVE!

Tom: Legend has it that the Phillie Phanatic was born on the Galapagos Islands and came to Philadelphia in 1978. No one knows the Phanatic's actual birthdate. The Phanatic's mom, Phoebe, might know but she's not talking.

In reality, the Phillie Phanatic was the love child born from the principles in this book. Bill Giles' mission of bringing fun back to baseball in Philadelphia led to the creation of the Phanatic. The talent and excellence that helped Bonnie Erickson create memorable characters, such as Miss Piggy, led her to design a wonderful costume for the Phillies. Dave Raymond, the first Phillie Phanatic, was the right guy for the job and brought that costume to life by giving the Phanatic heart and soul. The Phillies organization has made the Phanatic a centerpiece in their branding efforts and is committed to making the green guy the best mascot in sports.

Everyone has played a part in the creation of the Phillie Phanatic, including the fans who have loved the Phanatic back. The Phanatic has touched a lot of people so that's a lot of love bouncing back at him.

It boggles my mind to think of the number of positive impressions the Phillie Phanatic makes every time he is out spreading Phanatic love.

Millions of fans see him at Phillies games and on TV. People of all ages come to see him at local appearances or maybe catch a glimpse of his antics on the sports highlight shows or on a YouTube video. A young fan might encounter the Phanatic for the first time by reading one of his kid's books or see him at a school assembly. Maybe they never have seen the Phanatic in person, but they cuddle with a Phanatic doll at bedtime. That is a lot of impressions and a lot of smiles and laughter, too.

We talked earlier about the number of opportunities we have each day to make a positive impression. Think of the number of encounters you have with people every day. Think of the number of encounters you have every week, every month and every year. Now think of every one of those encounters as being a loving encounter. Making a positive impression with every encounter, every day is a goal that we all should work towards. Use positive words and high-five or fist bump a co-worker every once in a while. It will pump them up and fire you up, too. Take time out from answering emails to be there for someone who needs an ear to bend. Bring more play into everything you do. Have fun. Dance and celebrate your success.

Philadelphia is home to the most passionate fans in the country. There are plenty of Phillie Phanatics out there. People tell me all the time, *"I wish I had your job!"* The truth is, I wish every fan could have the opportunity to step into the Phanatic's oversized shoes at least once. It's a blast!

But now you *can* be the Phillie Phanatic. The best part about it is that you can be the Phanatic without stepping into a hot, furry costume. You don't have to endure the sweat, smell and the fur balls that occasionally get caught in my throat. You can be the Phanatic by living our *Pheel the Love!* principles every day. You can surround yourself with the same love, passion and energy that surrounds the Phanatic.

The Phanatic and the Phillies were showered with love at the World Championship parade in 2008. Millions of fans lined the street to get a glimpse of their heroes and to show their appreciation. It was an incredible feeling being on the receiving end of all of that love.

Now imagine that you are on one of those trucks rumbling down Broad Street. Imagine that those millions of fans are not Phillies fans but they are all the people that you've encountered throughout your lifetime. They are jumping for joy and showing you appreciation for sharing your love with them. Imagine their joy -- imagine how that would feel!

Evan: Tom and I were on the phone, having one of our planning sessions for the book. He was in Florida and driving to the ballpark for a spring training game. I knew he had arrived because I could hear the backup beeper in his van as we were talking. He apologized for having to get off the phone but he had to get to work. I asked if he had time for one more story.

That week I made a call to a client who heads up an honor society for college student leaders. I told her about the book we were writing. Little did I know that she is a huge Phanatic fan - another middle-aged professional who goes bunko for the Phanatic. I asked her why she loved the Phanatic and she described many of the principles in our book. She also talked about nostalgia. She said that every time she sees the Phanatic, childhood memories of spending time with her family come rushing back to her. She told me how her screen saver at work is either her children or the Phillie Phanatic. The love he engenders and the loyalty he inspires still amazes me.

Tom is used to this. It's his life and what he experiences all the time. Meeting Tom put me very close to someone who is at the core of this amazing loyalty. My organization works with many great organizations. We get close to their CEOs and upper management. We get to see what can happen when excellence is truly in the heart and soul of the people who create and run companies. It is so clear to us. All great companies we have either studied or worked with are brimming with the love we describe in this book. They may not use the word, "love" and most times, they don't realize that love is the essence of their greatness. However, to us it's simple – great companies commit to a higher purpose. While that purpose may be expressed differently in each organization, there is a common thread. Excellence. They are committed to excellence, to doing great things and to being special. It is non-negotiable for them. They have to do it that way. It is in their blood. It is what they love to do.

I feel the same way about Tom. As we have gotten to know and work with Tom, we realized that the Phanatic is not just a character he plays. He truly is like that. The love he gets is truly the love he gives. He exudes each of these principles. Not perfectly all of the time (ask his wife), none of us do, but his quotient of love is very high. It's authentic to who he is.

As I was relaying this story about my client's love for the Phanatic, I could feel Tom's focus shifting. He wasn't as present as he had been and I could hear him starting to feel rushed. I thought it was because he was at the ballpark and was shifting into work mode.

But then, I realized what was going on. *"Evan, I've got to go. Some fans have recognized me and want me to sign some autographs."*

Even though his van is unmarked, the fans had figured out who was inside. He didn't have his costume on yet, but they knew. I thought to myself, *"This is perfect. This is Tom doing his thing. We are not just writing about a theory; this love stuff is real. This is what great people and great organizations do."*

He had to go. It was time to go spread some love.

Thank you,
Tom and Evan

PHEEL *the* LOVE!

RESOURCES AT-A-GLANCE

PRINCIPLE #1
THE *big* SMOOCH!: LOVE *them* FIRST

PRINCIPLE #2
SEE THROUGH *your* CUSTOMER'S CAMERA: MAKE *every* ENCOUNTER COUNT

PRINCIPLE #3
DUCT TAPE *&* HOT DOGS: BE COMMITTED *to* OPERATIONAL EXCELLENCE

PRINCIPLE #4
THE BALLPARK *and* BEYOND: BRIDGE THE DIVIDE BETWEEN YOU *&* YOUR CUSTOMERS

PRINCIPLE #5
AVOID *the* WHAMMY!: PUT THE RIGHT PEOPLE IN *the* RIGHT POSITIONS

PRINCIPLE #6
GIVE'M *the* BELLY WHOMP: MAKE *it* FUN!

PRINCIPLE #7
7TH *inning* CELEBRATION: DANCE *and* BE OPTIMISTIC NO MATTER WHAT THE SCORE

RESOURCES AT-A-GLANCE

THE DNA *of* LOVE™
D = DECIDE
N = NOTICE
A = ACT

THE LEVERS *of* LOVE™
BE *kind*

BE *excellent*

THINK *love*

SPEAK *love*

RESOURCES AT-A-GLANCE

THE LOVE 15™

1. Do people love coming to work here? What do we have to do to create a workplace that people love?

2. Team members want their work to matter and have meaning. Is our business connected to a higher purpose? Does everyone understand what that higher purpose is?

3. Do our customers love our product or service? What can we do to help them love us more?

4. People love to be associated with excellence. As an organization, are we striving for excellence in everything we do? How can we be more excellent?

5. Love flourishes in an environment of respect. How do we ensure that everyone feels respected?

6. We all want to contribute and do our best. Does our culture encourage everyone to tap into their passion and fully utilize their talents?

7. Feeling valued is critical to fostering an environment of love. Do our people feel valued and well-compensated?

8. People like feeling a part of something. How can we create a more inclusive and collaborative environment?

9. People thrive when they are learning and progressing. How do we create more opportunities for people to learn and develop?

10. People are influenced by their physical environment. Is our space welcoming, inspiring and functional?

11. Everyone has unique skills, abilities and interests. Do we have the right people in the right positions?

12. People want to be "seen" and noticed. What can we do to make our team members and customers feel special?

13. Getting the chance to work with other well-meaning, high-performing people is exciting. What can we do to ensure that our organization is chock-full of smart, nice people?

14. Optimism is an awesome quality in any organization. To what extent are we optimistic in our attitude and actions?

15. What can we do to make our day and our interactions more fun and enjoyable?

BURGOYNE *and* MARCUS

NOTES

PHEEL *the* LOVE!

NOTES

NOTES

ABOUT *the* AUTHORS

TOM BURGOYNE

A certifiable Philadelphia sports nut, Tom started his life as the Phillie Phanatic in 1989 as the back-up to the original Phanatic, Dave Raymond, and took over as the game day Phanatic in 1994. Tom not only appears as the Phanatic at all Phillies home games, but has traveled around the country and around the world bringing the Phanatic's special brand of humor to sports fans everywhere. Tom is a prolific author and energetic speaker who encourages people to reach for the stars and make every moment count.

EVAN MARCUS

Evan has spent the last 25 years working hand-in-hand with leaders helping them to clarify their strategy, build powerful teams and overcome barriers to success.
A true teacher at heart, he coaches Executives on an individual and group basis. As a sought-out keynote speaker, Evan is on a mission to transform the world through business. He is also co-founder of the Sounding Board™, a prominent CEO group. A father of three boys, Evan meditates whenever he can—although his kids think it's code for "napping".

PHEEL *the* LOVE!

OTHER BOOKS BY TOM BURGOYNE

NON-FICTION

More than Beards, Bellies and Biceps:
The Story of the 1993 Phillies (And the Phillie Phanatic Too)

Movin' On Up:
Baseball and Philadelphia Then, Now, and Always

CHILDREN'S BOOKS

The Phillie Phanatic's Galapagos Gang

The Phillie Phanatic's Spring Training

The Phillie Phanatic's One-Man Band

The Phillie Phanatic's Hall of Fame Journey

The Phillie Phanatic's Friendly Games

The Phillie Phanatic's Philadelphia Story

The Phillie Phanatic's Galapagos Islands Adventure

The Phillie Phanatic's Christmas Wish

The Phillie Phanatic's Parade of Champions

Happy Birthday Phillie Phanatic

The Adventures of Super Phanatic

The Phillie Phanatic's Phantastic Journey

The Phillie Phanatic's Moving Day

The Phillie Phanatic's Happiest Memories

BOOK BY EVAN MARCUS

It's O.K. to Play:
30 Days to a Ridiculously Wonderful Life!

BRING
PHEEL *the* **LOVE!**
TO YOUR ORGANIZATION

PHEEL THE LOVE!™ KEYNOTE

In this world of fast-paced change, businesses everywhere are searching for the critical levers to ensure growth and sustainability. In this keynote speech:

✔ You'll learn how the Phillie Phanatic inspires fierce loyalty from his fans and drives revenue.

✔ You'll better understand the business case for love.

✔ You'll see the ways in which Phanatic inspired principles like "The Big Smooch" are already being applied by successful companies such as Vanguard, WAWA and Wegmans.

LOYAL, LOVING FANS
FOR LIFE!™ WORKSHOP

Customer loyalty is the holy grail of customer service. This workshop is perfect for people who want to WOW! their employees and their customers. You'll hit the ball out of the park when you discover how to create loyal, loving fans for life and how to foster Phillie Phanatic style love in your business.

This scalable 1/2-day to full-day session is ideal for individual service providers, line managers, and those in charge of corporate culture. Don't wait to schedule this workshop for your organization, it's a guaranteed home run!

Made in the USA
Columbia, SC
10 September 2021